ROSALIND FRANKLIN

A LIFE STORY

Michael Ford

Illustrated by **Mike Phillips**

■ SCHOLASTIC

Published in the UK by Scholastic Children's Books, 2020
Euston House, 24 Eversholt Street, London, NW1 1DB
A division of Scholastic Limited

London ~ New York ~ Toronto ~ Sydney ~ Auckland
Mexico City ~ New Delhi ~ Hong Kong

Text copyright © Michael Ford, 2020
Cover illustration by Sarah Papworth
Inside illustrations by Mike Phillips

ISBN 978 1407 19320 5

Printed and bound by CPI Group (UK) Ltd, Croydon, CR0 4YY

Papers used by Scholastic Children's Books are made from woods grown in
sustainable forests.

2 4 6 8 10 9 7 5 3 1

www.scholastic.co.uk

CONTENTS

THE BUILDING BLOCKS OF LIFE

DNA Discovery

In 1962, the Nobel Prize in Physiology or Medicine was awarded to three men: Maurice Wilkins, Francis Crick and James Watson. Through their work, they'd discovered one of life's mysteries – that biological information is stored and copied in cells in a complex molecule called deoxyribonucleic acid (DNA). This ground-breaking work earned them the most prestigious award in science and changed the way we looked at the human body, forever.

Today, the structure of DNA is a widely known image – a double helix, connected by horizontal bands. Imagine a ladder made of rubber that's twisted round. But in 1962, the structure of DNA was a revolutionary discovery, made less than ten years before.

Wilkins, Crick and Watson shared the Nobel Prize three ways but in different circumstances there could well have been another recipient. There had been another scientist heavily involved in the race to solve the mystery of the structure of DNA. From a young age, Rosalind Franklin had a passion for science and her drive and determination had led her to become a world-class expert in her field. It was her research that made the discovery possible.

A Man's World

Due to its tiny size, DNA is impossible to see with the naked eye, or even a microscope. It was thanks to Rosalind Franklin, through her expertise in a technique called X-ray crystallography – taking pictures with X-rays – that the other scientists confirmed its structure and finalized their theory about the way it functioned. It may sound like a small thing but scientific advancement is rarely a case of huge leaps in understanding. It creeps along by trial and error, theory and experiment, evidence and proof. It was Rosalind's fantastic pictures that allowed scientists to finally solve the mystery and cross the finish line.

So, why didn't Rosalind Franklin win the Nobel Prize? The fact she didn't receive recognition at the time is best described as a mixture of bad luck – by the time the Nobel Committee awarded its prize, Rosalind had died – and prejudice.

GENDER INEQUALITY

Until the 1960s, there were quite different expectations for men and women in political life and in the workplace. Women had only gained the right to vote in 1918 (and even then it was only women over the age of thirty who could vote) and the place they occupied in society was similarly repressed. There was a complicated mixture of cultural reasons for this, but the most obvious is that women were expected to get married, have children and stay at home. This meant that most women had children at a young age and afterwards remained in the home to care for them. Because this was the case, it affected the way girls were educated, with a focus on different subjects at school, and their potential career opportunities were limited.

Though women could attend university at the time, they could not officially earn a degree until the 1920s and many work spaces had separate areas for men and women.

In Rosalind's day, once a woman got married, it was common to not go back to work at all. When Rosalind was growing up, only around thirty per cent of women worked at all outside the home and once they had children, that figure fell rapidly.

Rosalind Franklin was one of very few women working in science, a field dominated by men. Though she must have experienced sexism, she never complained in her writings about it. On the other hand, the prejudiced attitudes of the time are clear in the words of many of the men who wrote about her. Rosalind was no pushover and would stick up for herself and her ideas. She made little effort to please others and saw herself as equal to any man working in her field. Perhaps because of this, some people found her hard to get on with at times and she made plenty of enemies in a fairly close-knit scientific community. As her own mother said later, "Rosalind's hates, as well as her friendships, tended to be enduring."

Rosalind Franklin's work involved looking at objects smaller than the eye can see but which have an important impact on the way we view the world and live in it. As well as unravelling the mysteries of DNA – the biological building blocks of life – she investigated the structure of coal, which at the time powered the world, and did pioneering work analysing plant viruses and later the infectious disease, polio. Her life story is one of a scientist constantly looking for answers, on a journey of discoveries.

THE FAMILY FRANKLIN

Rosalind Elsie Franklin was born on 25 July, 1920 at her family's house in Chepstow Villas, in Notting Hill, London. She came from a well-established Anglo-Jewish family. Over the course of several hundred years, waves of Jewish immigrants had travelled from continental Europe to England, often fleeing persecution. Rosalind's own ancestors had first arrived in the eighteenth century and since that time they had been senior figures in publishing, academia, the banking industry and politics.

Rosalind's father, Ellis Arthur, was a merchant banker, providing financial services to companies and the wealthy. Her mother, Muriel Frances, did not work, but stayed at home to look after the children and the house. They already had one child when Rosalind was born, a fifteen-month-old called David. Three more children would follow over the next nine years: Colin, Roland and Jenifer.

THE FRANKLIN FAMILY TREE

Grandparents (Rosalind's mother's side):
John Felix Waley
Ethel Esther Schloss (became Ethel Esther Waley)

Grandparents (Rosalind's father's side):
Arthur Ellis Franklin
Caroline Jacob (became Caroline Franklin)

Their children: Ellis Arthur, Mamie, Alice

Ellis Arthur married Muriel Frances Waley
Children:
David (born 1919)
Rosalind (born 1920)
Colin (born 1923)
Roland (born 1926)
Jenifer (born 1929)

In 1923, as the family grew, the Franklins moved to a larger house in nearby Pembridge Place. Rosalind's grandparents, along with many of her uncles, aunts and cousins, all lived within a mile or so. Nowadays, Notting Hill is an expensive and fashionable place to live but in the 1920s it was a bit shabbier, with quite a high rate of crime. The Franklins moved there because they could afford a bigger home, while staying near to their friends and relatives. Though the house was big, it was hardly modern: water still had to be fetched from a well in the street, rather than being pumped into the property.

Though the family were Jewish and Rosalind's grandfather had helped found a local synagogue, her day-to-day life was not a strictly religious upbringing. Her father's religious faith was important to him but Rosalind and her siblings did not attend the synagogue regularly.

Rosalind had a happy childhood. There was no shortage of food, they took regular holidays and could afford to educate their children privately. Her parents were loving and kind. They expected all their children to grow up into responsible members of the community, with good manners towards their elders. Rosalind's father, Ellis, believed strongly in the value of education and wanted his daughters to be taught subjects to the same level as his sons. He hoped that Rosalind and Jenifer would seek employment in whatever field they wished. Ellis had wanted to study physics at Oxford University but World War One had put an end to this ambition. He married his wife, Muriel, before heading off to fight in France as a captain in the King's Own Yorkshire Light Infantry Regiment. By the time the war ended, it was expected that as a married man he should find a job, rather than go to university, so he joined the bank, Keyser's, which was run by his wider family. As well as being a successful banker, Ellis worked with several charities alongside Muriel.

Rosalind's parents employed a live-in nanny, Ada Griffiths, to help look after the children. Rosalind and her siblings all had happy memories of Ada, who they knew as "Nannie". She joined the family after the birth of Rosalind's older brother, David, and lived with them long after the last of the children was born. It was her job to handle their day-to-day care: preparing their meals, mending clothes, solving squabbles and getting them to school on time. She taught Rosalind how to knit and sew. Jenifer recalls visiting Hyde Park – the largest of London's parks – walking past the balloon-seller and through Kensington Palace Gardens, listening to bands and meeting other nannies looking after their children. Nannie would occasionally go home to visit her own family in Shropshire and when she did Rosalind would miss her terribly.

She continued to write letters to Ada throughout her life.

Family Holidays

The pressures of five children to feed meant that the Franklins lived a thrifty day-to-day life, even though they employed maids as well as the nanny. Clothes were hand-me-downs and meals were frugal. Nothing was wasted and there were few treats. Rosalind certainly wasn't spoiled. However, one area in which Rosalind was lucky was the holidays she and her family took.

During the 1920s, the majority of people rarely travelled ten miles from where they were born but when Rosalind was young, the Franklins got out of London often, visiting destinations around the United Kingdom, such as the Isles of Scilly, the Cornish coast and South Wales. The family went on long hikes in the mountains and swam in the sea. Rosalind enjoyed these adventures and her love of the outdoors stayed with her throughout her life.

She also travelled to France at a young age; it was a country she fell in love with.

Rosalind regularly visited her grandparents – her father's father, Arthur Ellis, was quite rich! He had a townhouse in London and a country estate, called Chartridge Lodge, in Buckinghamshire. It had tennis courts, a croquet lawn, a five-car garage and a farm attached, as well as a large staff. Rosalind spent many weekends at Chartridge growing up and used to enjoy developing photos in the house's very own darkroom, with her brother, Colin. With her other siblings, she would spend hours in nature, collecting frogspawn, foraging for mushrooms or enjoying long walks in the surrounding countryside.

Though not naughty, Rosalind could be mischievous and battling for attention with three brothers gave her a determined and stubborn streak. Her mother Muriel wrote that "Rosalind enjoyed this trick of teasing — but with a burbling, mischievous delight, that, for anyone with a sense of fun, took the sting out of it." She also had a temper and was easily moved to tears by things she found unfair, often complaining that she thought her brothers were treated better than her. At a young age, her Aunt Mamie described her as "alarmingly clever" – both in the way she spoke and in her early grasp of mathematics.

Starting School

When she was five years old, Rosalind started at Norland Place, a private day school about a mile from her house. Unusually for the time, Norland Place educated boys and girls together, though boys only stayed until they were eight and girls until they were eleven. Rosalind studied literature, history and maths, in addition to less common subjects like woodwork. She took to lessons with determination and often with a competitive attitude, wanting to achieve top marks. There was little difference in the way boys and girls were taught at the school and Rosalind did well at sports too, particularly cricket and hockey. But maths was by far her favourite subject. Music was probably her weakest!

Rosalind left Norland Place early, at the age of nine, when her parents decided it would be better to send her to boarding school. Despite a happy childhood until that point, she had been the victim of several illnesses in her early years, including one infection that forced her to stay indoors and rest for several weeks. These were the sort of illnesses that children are vaccinated against today, or which doctors can easily treat, but in the 1920s it would mean a child spending long periods resting and recovering, and was often an anxious time for parents. Child mortality in 1920 was around eighty per thousand live births, so around one in every twelve children did not survive infancy.

Her parents believed that sea air would be an improvement on the smog and smoke of London, so they selected the Lindores School for Young Ladies near Bexhill in Sussex. The move coincided with the arrival of Rosalind's youngest sister, Jenifer. Later in life, Rosalind told people that she resented her parents for making the decision to send her away, believing it to be "completely unnecessary". It's hard to imagine how she must have felt, being removed from the life she knew in London, the friends from her school and the family she'd grown up with, including a new baby sister. Her letters home were full of questions about family life, including the new kitten living at Pembridge Place. Boarding school was still common for children of Rosalind's upper middle-class background, so she was at least surrounded by plenty of girls in a similar position.

Though Rosalind was homesick, she thrived in Sussex. She was healthy and did well in her studies, particularly science and maths subjects, including geometry, geology, chemistry and physics. She was often top of the class when marks were handed out and took great pleasure in the fact, proudly writing home to tell her parents. Sometimes she would even argue with her teachers about her marks, if she thought they'd calculated them wrongly! As well as continuing to play hockey, she became a strong swimmer – the school was only about half a mile from the seafront.

Rosalind threw herself into school life, getting involved in sports clubs and other after-school activities, but in some ways, she was still an outsider. Most of the girls at the school were Christians and attended the local church every Sunday. As a Jew, Rosalind did not accompany them, but was instead sent Hebrew lessons by her family in the post from London. She didn't always fully complete them, much to the annoyance of her parents.

She was an avid letter-writer throughout her life. Her parents expected regular reports from school and she also wrote often to her brother and sisters, her grandparents and her nanny, Ada.

Schoolgirl Scientist

After two years at Lindores, Rosalind returned to London to begin her secondary school education. Now eleven years old, her parents enrolled her at St Paul's in west London, one of the most prestigious private schools in England. Though the boys' school had been around since the sixteenth century, the girls' division had only been established in 1904. In fact, Rosalind's Aunt Mamie was one of the first female pupils there. Though the boys' and girls' school shared the same name, they were a few hundred metres from each other and they rarely mixed at all.

The school was not religious, which was rare for the time, but also made it a fitting environment for the children of Jewish families. Indeed, several of Rosalind's fellow students were cousins or more distant relatives. The school took girls from a variety of backgrounds, from all across London. The uniform and felt hat Rosalind wore each day were blue and made by the famous (and expensive) London clothing store, Daniel Neal.

At St Paul's, Rosalind met Jean Kerslake, who became a close friend for life. The two of them completed school projects together and helped each other with homework, as well as becoming patrol leaders in the Girl Guides. They both did well at gym and were often top of the class. Jean thought that Rosalind was adventurous and confident in her opinions. She came from a less wealthy background and found Rosalind's family and home in Pembridge Place intimidating, especially Rosalind's father, Ellis. But it was nothing compared to Rosalind's grandfather's estate in the country – a place several of Rosalind's St Paul's friends visited over the years, only to be amazed at its size.

Another life-long friend whom Rosalind met at St Paul's in her first year was Anne Crawford, who went on holiday to Wales with Rosalind's family during the summer holiday. She was surprised to find that the Franklins had enough money to take three maids on holiday, as well as hiring local help.

The headmistress at St Paul's – Miss Ethel Strudwick – believed that girls should be "prepared for a career", rather than a life stuck in the home. Previous students had gone on to all kinds of professional jobs in publishing, the civil service, medicine and law. There couldn't have been a better place for a driven student like Rosalind. From the start, she did well in maths and science, along with French, German and Latin. Rosalind played hockey, cricket and joined the tennis team as well.

Rosalind was always in the top section of the class and was awarded a scholarship in her first year – along with Anne Crawford – meaning the school would offer her parents reduced fees. However, Rosalind's mother and father refused, as it was against their principles to accept money they did not need. In their minds, it could go to someone more in need of the financial help.

Although she was academically gifted, Rosalind definitely wasn't a teacher's pet! She was already finding that her interests lay in science and made no attempt to disguise her feelings about other subjects. Literature, she found "dreary" and her appreciation of music was so bad that her music teacher suggested she have her hearing tested. Even her maths and science teachers noticed that she could appear argumentative at times, especially over the marks she was awarded (she once, in a letter to her sister, called her teacher an "old pig" when she felt hard done by).

Partly, her teachers' worries may simply have been because Rosalind wasn't a typical, quiet schoolgirl, as was expected then. She had grown up in a household where family discussion and disagreements were common – she was used to speaking her mind, even to adults. She also knew that praise and attention didn't come unless you earned them. Though she had her close friends, like Anne and Jean, she showed little interest in extending that circle or trying to please others. Her mother Muriel called it Rosalind's "walking alone" phase. In order to get their daughter to open up more, they bought her a kitten, which she named "Wilhelmina" or "Willy". The cat would sit on the arm of her chair as she did her homework.

After five years of general education at St Paul's, Rosalind was awarded her School Certificate at the age of sixteen. She then chose to study chemistry, physics and mathematics for her Higher School Certificate, unusual choices for a girl at this time. She was lucky that St Paul's had brand-new science facilities, where she spent much of her time, but even at this stage of her education the differing expectations for girls and boys were apparent. Girls were not allowed the same access to the laboratories in their free periods and their teachers emphasized neatness in their work and thorough note-keeping, rather than bold experimentation or new ideas.

One rare occasion on which the boys and girls of St Paul's mixed was a school dance. It wasn't a happy occasion for Rosalind. She and Jean went together, but no one danced with them all evening. Rosalind blamed her outfit – a short taffeta party dress that she thought made her look very young. The rest of the girls were wearing floor-length evening dresses and some of them even had make-up on which Rosalind's mother would never allow.

Trouble in Europe

The final year of Rosalind's schooling in 1938, coincided with dark events in continental Europe. Hitler was rising to power and anti-Jewish hate speech and violence were on the rise.

As a result of the events in Europe, waves of Jewish refugees began to arrive in Britain, looking for shelter and work. As a Jewish family, the Franklins were eager to offer assistance. Ellis reduced his working hours at the bank to help out with the daunting task of welcoming refugees and other members of the family did their bit in the rehoming effort too. The headmistress at St Paul's allowed Rosalind and her friends to join the mission, helping with filing and other administrative duties at Woburn House, which was the headquarters to the Jewish Refugee Committee. Some Jewish arrivals had relatives in Britain who could support them, but many were not so fortunate. Among the immigrants were thousands of children from Nazi-occupied territories, who arrived unaccompanied on the *Kindertransport*.

KINDERTRANSPORT

Nine months prior to the outbreak of World War Two, a relief effort named *Kindertransport* (which is German for "children's transport") took place. During this relief effort, a handful of countries took in predominantly Jewish children from Nazi Germany and Nazi-occupied Austria, Czechoslovakia and Poland. The UK was one of the countries that joined the relief force, along with Holland, Belgium and France, and took in nearly 10,000 children who were placed in British foster homes, schools and farms.

There is a sculpture, *Kindertransport – The Arrival*, currently in Liverpool Street station, London. It was installed in 2006 to commemorate the arrival of the 10,000 Jewish children who were seeking refuge.

Rosalind's own family took in two children. One of them was called Evi Eisenstadter. She was nine years old when she arrived in the summer of 1938, after her father was imprisoned in the Buchenwald concentration camp in Germany. On her arrival, Evi was taken by the chauffeur of Rosalind's grandfather straight to the grand Chartridge estate, where the family were staying for the weekend. It was quite a shock for the little Austrian girl. When she saw Rosalind's grandfather, Arthur, coming down the stairs in evening wear, she thought he must be the king!

Off to University

It's hardly surprising that Rosalind wanted to study science at university, nor that she chose the best university in the country for science at that time. Halfway through her final year at school, she visited the University of Cambridge to sit the entrance exams for physics and chemistry. As she so often had been at school, she was obsessed with the marks she got in her papers and worried about how she had performed in the tests. Would her marks be enough to get a place? Entrance to Cambridge was based partly on the written tests and partly on an interview. Rosalind's worries were unfounded, because she not only got top marks in the chemistry exam, she also performed well in the interview.

There were only two Cambridge colleges at the time that allowed women to enrol: Girton and Newnham. She was offered a place at both and accepted the Newnham offer. As Rosalind was only eighteen, and most women entered the university at nineteen, the college suggested she wait a further year to enrol as she would have a greater chance of receiving a scholarship. Jean Kerslake chose this option but Rosalind didn't want to wait – science was calling on her.

CAMBRIDGE

After completing her final year at St Paul's, she was offered a School Leaving Exhibition (an annual sum of money) of thirty pounds, in recognition of her hard work and future potential. At the time it was a considerable amount, equivalent to about £2,000 today. But as with her earlier offer of scholarship from the school, her father refused the money on her behalf.

WOMEN AT CAMBRIDGE

Cambridge University has existed as an institution of learning since the beginning of the thirteenth century but only began to admit women in 1869, seventy years before Rosalind's arrival. Even with the founding of the two female-only colleges, the young women were still not accepted as full members of the university in the same way as the men. They were not called "undergraduates", because they were not allowed to graduate officially (that is, get a degree).

Girton and Newnham between them accepted around 500 women in 1938, about a tenth of the university's male student population. Cambridge had never had a female professor in its seven-hundred-year history, though during Rosalind's time there, it appointed its first: the archaeologist, Dorothy Garrod.

Rosalind was eager to focus on the opportunities the university offered. And there were many. She was surrounded for the first time in her life by others focused on the topic she loved. She was living away from home, with freedom and her own money to spend. She wrote to her father about her purchases of a second-hand chair, an old bicycle to get around, used textbooks and an annual membership of the Chemical Society, rather than a monthly one, which saved her six shillings. And though the attitudes of the university arose from old-fashioned beliefs about the sexes, young men and women were not kept apart in the same way they had been at school. She had male teachers and male fellow students. Lectures and labs were open to all. However, the women still had to sit separately and weren't allowed to wear the ornate robes of male students, although the education they received was largely the same.

Outside the ceremonial and formal practices of the university, Rosalind was free to do the same things as other students: eat out, shop for furniture for her room, use the library and go boating on the River Cam. The things she expressed a dislike for in her letters home didn't have much to do with being a woman in a predominantly male institution, but social events that used up her time – college dining events, Jewish society obligations. She wrote that Newnham was in many ways like a boarding school, though she had her own room in the college halls of residence, rather than sharing. One thing she particularly hated was being forced to take part in a college first-year play on the same night as two famous scientists were giving a talk at the Cambridge Union.

A Serious Student

Rosalind had come to Cambridge for science and she approached her studies with passion, grasping all the academic possibilities she could. Though her core courses were chemistry, physics and maths, she also studied mineralogy. She took a module in German as well, because at the time that country produced a great deal of scientific literature in her field. She joined a mathematics society called the Archimedeans (named after the famous ancient Greek mathematician Archimedes) and attended many lectures not strictly within her subjects, including zoological talks on penguins and whales.

The University of Cambridge was a top institution in both physics and mathematics, with many famous figures in the subjects having studied there. Its laboratory facilities were second-to-none and a big step up from the labs at St Paul's. Rosalind had to quickly learn new and complicated laboratory techniques, like how to clean and assemble apparatus.

One of the early talks she went to was hosted by Professor William Lawrence Bragg, known as a pioneer in the technique called "X-ray crystallography". In essence, this involved trying to work out the structure of crystals using X-rays and would later be the focus of Rosalind's career.

WILLIAM LAWRENCE BRAGG

X-RAYS AND CRYSTALS

X-rays are a sort of electromagnetic radiation, just like normal light. Light from the sun, or a lightbulb, lets us see things by bouncing off them and into our eyes. X-rays have a higher energy and because of this, they can pass through objects. X-rays have different uses. The one we all know of is used to look inside human bodies, but scientists can also use them to look inside other materials, such as crystals, which are substances or materials formed by a collection of atoms ordered into a repeating, regular pattern.

Not all Rosalind's lessons and lectures were a success. She wasn't shy about criticizing certain tutors she felt weren't very good at their jobs, or who had a poor understanding of science. She would switch the lectures she attended to find the best teachers she could. Her social life was much the same as at school. She had few close friends and chose not to join in with many social activities. She was at her happiest when spending long hours in the lab, carrying out practical experiments. She continued, however, to take an interest in sports, playing squash, as well as going on long cycling rides. Occasionally, she cycled almost ninety kilometres from Cambridge back to her parents' home in Pembridge Place. Though her mother worried about her having an accident, Rosalind was unafraid. She didn't wear a helmet, but luckily there were far fewer cars on the road at that time!

A Rising Tension

Rosalind's immediate day-to-day life at Cambridge – the studying, the sports and the societies – were all taking place against a bigger backdrop of global politics. No one could avoid the growing tensions in Europe that would soon erupt into World War Two. Newspapers of the time were full of stories about Germany's aggression. Politics seeped into Cambridge in the form of lectures and political meetings but the majority of the students and staff at the university leant towards pacifism, the belief that war should be avoided at all costs. People struggled to accept that war was coming, at least on a scale that would affect Great Britain, and many were able to overlook Adolf Hitler's actions or at least push them to the back of their mind.

Rosalind had a different attitude than many of her fellow students and it was largely due to her upbringing. Dreadful stories of violence directed towards Jews in Germany appeared in British newspapers and these touched Rosalind. But there were also people in Britain who agreed with the Nazis. A march in support of Hitler and his policies paraded through London, led by Oswald Mosley and his British Union of Fascists. The rising tide of anti-Semitism struck Rosalind and her family deeply. At around the same time, the Prime Minister of Great Britain, Neville Chamberlain, was restricting refugee immigration, limiting the numbers of Jews who could seek safety in Britain. To Rosalind and others, it looked like Britain was washing its hands of the problems in Europe and pulling up the drawbridge to those who most needed the country's help.

But studying was still the most important thing in Rosalind's life. Her childhood worries about exams and marks had not left her. She was bad at managing her time in test papers, often getting stuck into some problems at the expense of others. She generally underestimated her performance in tests, only to be pleasantly surprised when the results came in. Typically, she felt her end-of-first-year exams at Cambridge had gone terribly, particularly her physics test. She predicted she would get a "Third" – the lowest pass mark that could be awarded at the university. It turned out to be a "Second" in that paper. But she had excelled in maths and chemistry and this meant a "First" overall. In fact, she got the second-highest mark in her year and was accepted to continue her studies in the sciences.

The Outbreak of War

In August 1939, during the university summer break, Rosalind was on holiday with her family, in Norway. All four of her siblings and her former nanny, Ada, were there too, enjoying hiking in the fresh air, fishing in the fjords and climbing over glaciers, roped together. Towards the end of their trip, a dramatic announcement cut their holiday short. Germany and the USSR had signed the Molotov–Ribbentrop Pact (named after the foreign ministers of each government), which stated that the two countries would not be enemies in any coming conflict. This was widely seen as a preparation for Germany to invade countries on its border. The Franklins travelled to the port of Bergen as quickly as they could, catching one of the last ferries across the ocean, before all non-essential travel was banned.

WORLD WAR TWO

After World War One had ended in 1918, the great nations of the world believed such a terrible slaughter could never happen again. They were wrong. Just over twenty years later, a number of different factors combined to ignite a second global conflict. The most obvious reason for the outbreak of war was the aggression of Adolf Hitler's Nazi party in Germany. Hitler rose to power in a Germany that felt harshly punished by the treaties that followed World War One.

He convinced the people that it was time to fight back and in September 1939 invaded the neighbouring country of Poland. This brought the USSR and Great Britain into the war and the conflict soon grew to encompass most of the European nations and later the United States of America. When the war finally ended in 1945, somewhere between seventy and eighty-five million people had died due to the conflict.

Back in England, Ellis Franklin made it clear that he expected all his children to seek employment in the war effort. He wanted them to put themselves to use in the service of their country. David left his studies at Oxford and Colin would later join the navy in 1942. Rosalind was happy to do her bit too, but she didn't want to waste her talents doing any old work. She wanted to have enough expertise to do something useful in the scientific fields in which she was learning so much. It made sense, therefore, to return to her studies in Cambridge. She and her father clashed over the decision, which was made more awkward because she still relied on his financial help. At first, he even refused to pay. Both father and daughter were forceful characters, unused to backing down, but in this case, Rosalind, her mother and her aunt worked together to convince him.

Specialist Science

Back in Cambridge, a period that became known as the "Phoney War" began, in which everyone expected Germany to begin a campaign of bombing but in fact things remained peaceful. The city was surrounded by airfields and it was believed that the Germans could very well send bomber planes to attack them. The university wanted its students to be ready and so air-raid drills were common and everyone had to carry gas masks around with them all the time. An alarm would sound, often at night and everyone would have to drop what they were doing, or climb out of bed and make their way to shelters dug into the college grounds. Rosalind, as a warden, was required to make sure her small group was present and correct. She thought it was all a waste of time and once refused to take part. When her hall of residence tutor, Susan Palmer, realized Rosalind was missing, she came to find her and told her off, calling her "disloyal, deceitful and untrustworthy". Rosalind argued back and the two became enemies. Rosalind resented spending hours on such activities when she could have been working in the lab.

Despite the frequent interruptions, Rosalind began to focus on the subjects that she would become famous for. She studied optics – how light of various wavelengths passes through lenses and objects – and learned about atomic chemistry. Though she wasn't a student of biological sciences, she researched the chemical properties of nucleic acids contained in chromosomes – some of the smallest building blocks of life in human cells. She became acquainted with the new face of crystallography, John Bernal. Her notebooks at the time show carefully labelled diagrams and contain a note that it might be possible to use X-ray crystallography to uncover the secrets of genetic inheritance – how physical features, such as eye colour, are passed from parent to child.

JOHN BERNAL (1901–1971)

Bernal was an Irish scientist who studied under William Henry Bragg and who used X-ray crystallography to look at the structure of organic molecules (that is, molecules relating to living things). At the age of 26, he was made the first lecturer in Structural Crystallography at Cambridge and he became the assistant director of Cambridge's famous Cavendish Laboratory in 1934.

War and Faith

Rosalind, like most of the other female students at Cambridge, remained at the university at the start of the war. The same could not be said for the male student population, which almost halved. Some went off to fight in the armed forces and others were drawn into other jobs relating to the war effort against Germany. There were a number of German students at Cambridge and they were interned (temporarily imprisoned) as potential threats to the country. It must have made the university feel very quiet and rather different, as there were now only five men to every woman, rather than ten.

Women – particularly those of a scientific background – were valued for their expertise and government ranks began to fill with ex-students from the women's colleges at Cambridge.

Though the treatment of Jews in Europe troubled Rosalind, she felt that some of the actions of the British were almost as shocking. She wasn't romantic about the war and she had little time for propaganda or stories of glory. As Germany invaded Holland, then Belgium and finally France, Rosalind was not at all hopeful. When Paris fell and the British army was forced to retreat from continental Europe via the beaches of Dunkirk, it looked very much like Rosalind was right to be pessimistic.

DUNKIRK

During World War Two, between 26 May and 4 June 1940, there was an evacuation in Dunkirk in which Allied soldiers were rescued from the beaches and harbour. The operation started after large numbers of Belgian,

British and French troops were cut off and surrounded by German troops. A massive relief effort was swiftly organized and by the end of the eighth day, 338,226 soldiers had been rescued by a fleet of over 800 boats, many of them captained by ordinary sailors rather than by Royal Navy officers. This evacuation effort was codenamed **"Operation Dynamo"**.

These views again brought Rosalind into conflict with her father, who was more straightforwardly patriotic. He believed that Britain represented all that was right and good and would prevail in the war because of those values. When Rosalind questioned those values, he didn't like it. But it was typical of Rosalind's character – she thought about science and the war in the same way. She observed carefully, trying to keep herself detached and unemotional about what she was seeing, before reaching a conclusion.

The arguments with her father about the rights and wrongs of the war and his anxiety about her choice of career, also came down to a clash between faith and science. Ellis accused Rosalind of having a "one-sided outlook" and thinking that science had the answers to everything. But for Rosalind, there could be no belief without evidence. Rosalind had never been a very religious person. She didn't believe in a creator God or that human beings were special, whereas these things were important to her more traditional Jewish father. It was still a time when marrying within the Jewish faith was seen as important for many Jewish families, to preserve the religious culture. All of Rosalind's siblings went on to marry other Jews and Ellis Franklin may have been worried about his oldest daughter's future marriage prospects if she moved away from the faith.

The war and Cambridge life continued. During her break, Rosalind took a walking holiday with her cousin, Ursula Franklin, to the Lake District (travelling to Europe at this time would have been unthinkable).

German bombs did begin to fall on the British mainland – in what became known as "the Blitz" – but Cambridge was mostly spared. Rosalind's parents weren't as lucky. Their house at Pembridge Place wasn't hit directly, but a house behind was, killing two people. Ellis and Muriel decided to move out of central London.

THE BLITZ

The Blitz, named after the German word for "lightning", was the German bombing campaign against Britain in 1940 and 1941, during World War Two. Hitler's airforce, the *Luftwaffe*, targeted London and industrial targets like factories and ports in other towns and cities.

From 7 September 1940, London was bombed for fifty-six out of the following fifty-seven days and nights. Though the attacks took place mostly at night, the planes sometimes flew over in the daytime as well.

Britain's own Royal Air Force succeeded in shooting down many of the German bomber planes, but the damage inflicted was still severe. More than 40,000 people were killed by *Luftwaffe* bombing during the war, almost half of them in the capital. Tens of thousands of houses were reduced to rubble.

As Rosalind entered her third year, more and more students and teachers were leaving to help with the war effort, including large numbers of scientists. It only added to the empty feeling, with whole departments and labs understaffed.

A New Interest

Rosalind began to specialize in an area of science called "physical chemistry", a branch of chemistry that applies the techniques and theories of physics. As she had previously, she sought out the best supervisor (a sort of teacher to guide her studies) to help her, a man called Fred Dainton. At first, he said his schedule was full and refused but Rosalind persisted and won him over.

Rosalind also went to a talk by a woman who would be a great influence in her life – the French-Jewish scientist Adrienne Weill.

ADRIENNE WEILL

Weill had fled from Nazi-occupied France, along with her daughter and now worked at Cavendish Laboratory, a physics research centre at Cambridge. Weill gave lectures in her native language, French (which Rosalind understood well enough to follow), in which she talked about her work under her own teacher, the physicist and chemist Marie Curie. As well as being an accomplished scientist and communicator, Weill was elegant, confident and liked to talk about politics in a serious way – she was a perfect role model for young Rosalind.

MARIE CURIE

Marie Curie (1867–1934) was a Polish scientist who conducted pioneering research on radioactivity. She was the first woman to win a Nobel Prize and the first person to win two, in two different scientific fields, physics and chemistry. She was also the first woman to become a professor at the University of Paris. Born in Warsaw, Poland, she is best known for coining the term radioactivity and discovering two elements, polonium and radium.

During World War One she developed X-ray technology that could be used in hospitals on the battlefield.

Marie Curie was aged sixty-six when she died in France in 1934 of an illness relating to exposure to radiation in the course of her work.

The German bombing of London only grew worse in early 1941 and with Rosalind halfway through her final year, her attention turned to what she might do afterwards. The war effort was taking its toll on the whole country. One outcome of so many men being involved in the war effort was that more women were recruited to the workforce. Jobs which had traditionally been occupied by men, in fields like industry and science, opened up to women for the first time. Rosalind, like many of the other women at the two Cambridge colleges, was signed up to a register at the government Appointments Board. This was intended to assign bright students to various jobs in the war effort, such as signalling or code-breaking, or to use their specialisms in engineering, geography or mapping and a host of other subjects. Rosalind, who loved her studies, wanted to stay on at the university but to do that she would have to pass her final exams with good marks.

As usual, she was desperately nervous. The nerves made her unable to sleep properly and she caught a cold during the exam period. Tired and ill, Rosalind struggled to manage her time during the test. Though she came top of her year in the physical chemistry paper, she failed to finish the other examinations, spending too much time answering the early questions in great detail and so running out of time. However, she still achieved a high enough mark for a Second Class degree and it was enough for Newnham College to award her a scholarship of fifteen pounds. Her potential was recognized by the

Government's Department of Scientific and Industrial Research too. It gave her a grant to continue research at the university.

During Rosalind's time at Cambridge, she had transformed from a promising student into a skilled scientist. She had learned the fundamental principles of laboratory work and a wide range of scientific topics. Most of all, she had direction. She knew that her future lay in physical chemistry – the unseen, but not unseeable, mechanisms of atoms and molecules.

A CAREER BECKONS

Rosalind's fourth year started badly. The college tutor whom she'd argued with about the air-raid drills, Susan Palmer, gave her a smaller room. Realizing she couldn't win this fight, Rosalind took action, choosing to move out into a house on her own. She was assigned to a new supervisor at Emmanuel College, Ronald George Wreyford Norrish. He was a grumpy man – whose own wife and children had moved to Devon to be far away from any bombing – and he was known to treat his juniors bossily and badly. Rosalind wrote that,

"HE'S THE SORT OF PERSON WHO LIKES YOU ALL RIGHT AS LONG AS YOU SAY YES TO EVERYTHING HE SAYS..."

A science supervisor directs his or her student in what to research, often to contribute to a larger area of study in which the supervisor specializes. The work Norrish asked Rosalind to do on his behalf related to how acid molecules combine into a larger structure called a "polymer". It didn't interest Rosalind greatly and she hated the fact the work she was doing had nothing to do with the war effort. Other friends from her school days were now involved in jobs directly related to fighting Hitler: Anne Crawford was working at the Bristol Aircraft Corporation, Jean Kerslake was involved in code-breaking and her cousin Ursula had joined the Auxiliary Territorial Service, the women's branch of the British Army.

But Rosalind approached her own work diligently and soon revealed that some of Norrish's theories were wrong. Science moves in steps, often two forward and one back. Disproving theories is as important to the process as proving them. Still, it must have been hard for Norrish to hear from someone younger and less experienced than him that the work he had assigned her wasn't finding the answers he wanted. But Rosalind was never the sort of person to hide from the truth – she faced facts head-on.

She and Norrish had a heated argument. He refused to read her notes and ordered her to carry out the experiments again in hope of different results. She refused. From that moment on, their relationship was strained, although he did give her a new project to work on.

The conflict with her father was never far from the surface either and it came up again as the summer of 1942 approached. Rosalind wanted to remain at Cambridge and continue to study for a PhD. But Ellis felt like she was avoiding war work and needed to do her duty in serving the country. Rosalind was annoyed. She wanted to help with the war effort – she had hoped Norrish would provide her with a study that would help the country; it wasn't her fault that he hadn't. But again, she wasn't willing to do any old job. Rosalind was young and very ambitious. She had been working hard for several years in a field she loved. To give it up at this stage and put the brakes on her learning was unthinkable to her.

At the same time, her social circle at the university was changing. Rosalind had never made friends easily with her fellow students and postgraduate colleagues but Adrienne Weill had introduced her to a group of French refugee students who all lived together in a hostel. Rosalind found talking with them more interesting than her English acquaintances at the university, though her own conversational French wasn't quite good enough to keep up. At the end of the summer term, just as she turned twenty-two, she moved in with them.

Joining the War Effort

She was still wondering whether to continue at Cambridge, or to try to find a job that aided the war effort, when the decision was made for her. The Ministry of Labour ruled that all female science research students were being called for military service. This didn't mean fighting on the front line but employing their skills in war work of various sorts. To Rosalind's surprise, Norrish suggested she appeal the decision in order to stay on at university. It seems he did privately value her work and expertise, even if he didn't act like it most of the time. But Rosalind had no intention of remaining under his supervision and so joined a government research laboratory based in Kingston-upon-Thames, just outside London. It was important for her to remain doing lab work, to be prepared for a real job after the war. She moved again, to a house in Putney Common, which she shared with her cousin Irene and a friend. They volunteered as air-raid wardens, which involved patrolling the neighbourhood to make sure people were safe before, during and after bombing attacks. They wore tin hats and used to walk or cycle the streets. Irene said she thought Rosalind was very brave in the way she'd march across Putney Common while the bombs fell.

Rosalind's fearless streak was also clear from the energetic and sometimes dangerous holidays she took at the time. She went away on separate trips with both Jean Kerslake and Anne Crawford, to the hills of North Wales, climbing the highest peaks in all weathers.

Mining the Secrets of Coal

In Kingston, Rosalind began a job as an Assistant Research Officer at the British Coal Utilisation Research Association (BCURA). It was a newly formed government-backed organization, whose job it was to investigate the uses and properties of coal. BCURA were looking for talented and ambitious PhD students and Rosalind fit the bill.

At the end of 1943, Rosalind's living arrangements changed once more. Her cousin Irene married and moved out and Rosalind herself suffered another bout of jaundice, a condition that causes yellow pigmentation of the skin and whites of the eyes. She chose to move back in with her family for a while. Once recovered, she commuted each day to Kingston from her parents' home.

THE ROLE OF COAL

It's hard for us to grasp now how important coal was in the 1940s. In 2019, the six remaining coal-fired power stations in the UK produced less than 5% of all electricity used in the UK (we now produce electricity using gas, nuclear and renewable sources) but in 1940, almost ninety per cent of our energy derived from coal. It heated our homes in open fires, powered trains and ships and had numerous industrial uses. The coal industry employed around 700,000 people (today it's around 2,000).

Coal is made when layers and layers of organic (carbon-based) plant-life are compressed under the Earth's surface over millions of years. The pressure and heat turn that organic carbon into inorganic carbon – the hard, black material we call coal. But the way the coal is formed causes different types to have different properties, in the way it burns, absorbs water and gases, and crucially, in the amount of energy it produces. For a country reliant on coal for energy, there could hardly have been a more important area of study.

Rosalind's work at BCURA mostly involved looking at the structure of coal at a molecular level, which she determined by passing different gases though it to measure what is called "porosity" – how easily a substance can absorb liquids or gases. Her particular skills at preparing and handling apparatus, designing experiments and measuring results, meant her time at BCURA (almost four years) was very productive. While she was there, Rosalind conducted original research into different types and properties of coal and she became a recognized expert in the field. She also made progress on research to use towards her PhD thesis for Cambridge.

It was the first time she was carrying out work fairly independently. Of course, she had superiors at BCURA but they weren't supervisors like she'd had at university. There, she was the principal scientist in her field and her time at BCURA gave her the confidence that she was on a career path. It also fulfilled her father's wishes that she do something for the benefit of her country. Though her parents didn't understand the details of her research (indeed, few people would have), they understood the importance of coal and they were proud of her work. She had proved to her father especially that her time at Cambridge had been worthwhile.

End of an Era

The war ended in 1945 while Rosalind was still working at BCURA. It brought her brother Colin home from service abroad. The country began to readjust to normal, peacetime life. Her friend and mentor Adrienne Weill returned to a liberated Paris and Rosalind submitted her PhD thesis. Though Norrish still wanted her to return to Cambridge, she rejected the offer due to her personal dislike for him and because it would have seemed a backwards step in her career.

The year 1945 was not only a milestone in global politics but also in women's place in science. The war, which had called so many men away, had enabled female scientists to show their expertise more than ever before, and it was in 1945 that women were first admitted to the Royal Society. Though women in science were still vastly outnumbered by men, there had been no better time in history for a female scientist to be at the start of her career.

THE ROYAL SOCIETY

The Royal Society was a group of leading scientists founded in the seventeenth century during the reign of Charles II. It is the oldest national scientific institution in the world and still exists today.

The first members, who were all men, included the likes of Sir Isaac Newton, who wrote foundational theories of motion and gravity. The Society's motto is the Latin phrase, *Nullius in verba*, which translates as "Take nobody's word for it". Members sought to prove scientific theories through observation and experimentation.

The two women admitted in 1945 were involved in similar fields to which Rosalind Franklin would later be drawn: Kathleen Lonsdale, a crystallographer, and Marjory Stevenson, a chemical microbiologist.

Rosalind was awarded her PhD that year. Having rejected Cambridge and growing restless at BCURA, she published her first paper in a scientific journal, written with her boss at BCURA, Donald H Bangham. Over the next few years, she published many more papers in collaboration with other scientists, as well as on her own. But for the time being, she needed a new job.

In the summer of 1946, with continental Europe once more accessible, Rosalind went on another long hiking holiday with her school friend Jean Kerslake. Always an adventurer, Rosalind chose the French Alps, where they climbed huge peaks with ice axes, crampons and ropes. She visited Adrienne Weill on the way south through the country. Rosalind had previously written to Weill asking if she knew of any employment she could take up. Ever since holidaying in France as a girl, Rosalind had loved the country: its culture, its people and its food. She had always spoken the language quite well and her friendship with Weill helped her improve.

After returning, Rosalind, Jean and another friend showed two French crystallography students around London when they visited for a conference on carbon hosted by the Royal Institution. One of the visitors was Marcel Mathieu, a friend of Adrienne Weill; the other was a man called Jacques Mering.

Though she was still only in her mid-twenties, Rosalind was not impressed by the conference and stood up in the audience to correct a prominent scientist called Harry Carlisle during his talk. His measurements were wrong, she declared. He later said he found her "abrupt". She was gaining a reputation of being honest – to the point of rudeness sometimes – especially when she knew she was right!

One person who was obviously impressed by her manner, though, was Marcel Mathieu, who ran an X-ray crystallography laboratory in France. A few weeks after the carbon conference, Rosalind received an offer of a job studying coal in Paris.

The Paris Years

The job was at Laboratoire Central Des Services Chimiques de l'État, a government laboratory researching industrial uses of chemistry. Twenty-six-year-old Rosalind was one of fifteen researchers working under Jacques Mering. Impressed with her work and expertise, he asked her to use a technique called X-ray diffraction to look at the molecular structure of charcoal and coal. Rosalind took to the work like a duck to water, learning how different sorts of coals responded to heat internally. Though the work had its uses, there was no specific end-goal in mind – this was science for science's sake.

X-RAY DIFFRACTION

In X-ray diffraction, X-rays are fired at a substance. The rays are diffracted (or bent) around the atoms inside the substance and hit a photographic plate behind. By measuring the pattern on the plate, scientists can determine how the atoms in the substance are arranged.

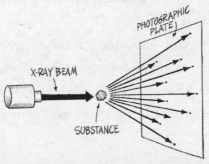

Upon first arriving in Paris, Rosalind lived in a rented apartment on the top floor of a building in the 6th *arrondissement*. South of River Seine, this *arrondissement* contains the famous Jardin de Luxembourg, a huge area of parkland and gardens, where Rosalind would go walking. It was a large apartment and though it wasn't as glamorous as where she'd grown up, it was cheap. The building had a single shared bathroom that she was permitted to use once a week (most of the time she washed with cold water in a tin bowl).

The apartment could get very cold in the winter and although there was a fireplace, wood was hard to come by. Rosalind, however, had never shied away from a lack of comfort – on her hiking and mountaineering holidays she was used to sleeping on floors in hostels, or the decks of ships. Her parents worried about her being all alone in a foreign country, but she reassured them she was fine.

Food was still "rationed" at this time, meaning that certain foods like meat, dairy products and flour were limited. Compared to London, the shortage was worse in Paris, where many food products were too expensive because the country's farms had been destroyed between 1940 and 1945. Rosalind often requested food parcels from her visitors, including things such as tea, jam and drinking chocolate.

There was a maid who cleaned the apartment and Rosalind got on well with her. The landlady, however, was another matter: Madame Dumas was grumpy and strict about the number of guests Rosalind could have. She had a small circle of friends, mostly connected with the lab in some way or other and they often ate together at local cafes.

Here men and women were not separated in the same way as at Cambridge – they mixed all the time. There were fewer traditional attitudes as well. A large number of the other staff at the lab were atheists (meaning they didn't believe in God or go to church) or socialists (people who think the government should split money more evenly among people in society, rather than it remaining in the hands of a wealthy few). The atmosphere was supportive and Rosalind found her colleagues refreshingly open-minded.

As well as working hard at the lab, Rosalind enjoyed swimming at the local pool and in the River Seine. Sometimes she went dancing in the evenings and on weekends she went on walking trips to the forests outside the capital or visited labs in other European cities. She went everywhere around the city by bicycle, as she found travelling underground on the Metro trains suffocating. Thrust into a French-speaking environment, she quickly became fluent. In many ways, she'd never felt at home in England, but now, in Paris, she found her place. Her family came over, in small groups, to visit. She was keen to show off her new life, cooking French dishes for her mother in her flat and taking her to the theatre and art exhibitions. Her brother, Colin, and sister, Jenifer, visited together and were treated to lunch at a local café where Rosalind's lab friends frequently ate. She also returned to London several times over the next few years, to visit friends and for the weddings of her brothers; David (1947), Roland (1949) and Colin (1950). She disliked the ferry crossing, which made her seasick and so chose to travel by plane.

Living and working alongside scientists (an Italian

X-ray crystallographer, Vittorio Luzzati, moved in next door with his wife) meant that the main topics of conversation, even outside the labs, turned into long discussions and arguments about the atomic structures of materials. For Rosalind, who always struggled with small talk, it was a happy time to have the lines between work and play so blurred. Under Jacques Mering, she flourished. She also met an English-speaking woman called Anne Sayre, wife of an American crystallographer. They became such good friends that Anne Sayre would later go on to write a biography of Rosalind, entitled *Rosalind Franklin and DNA*.

Though she was falling in love with France, Rosalind didn't lose all her affection for her homeland. She still listened to the BBC on her wireless and subscribed to English journals and magazines. Even though she had more freedom in France than she'd ever had before, Rosalind always planned to head back to London at some point.

What France offered was the chance to

research and publish papers, which would enhance her reputation and job prospects upon her return. While at the Laboratoire, Rosalind had five papers on the structures of coal accepted for publication. The papers were short, with complicated mathematical equations and diagrams, but they made Rosalind an up-and-coming scientific figure. She also took part in seminars and conferences across France, where she met other scientists from around the world.

While the conclusions of her research were meticulous and well argued, the work itself required Rosalind to get her hands dirty. X-ray diffraction involves directing a beam of X-rays through a vacuum tube at the material one wants to analyse and it was Rosalind's job to build, maintain and clean the apparatus, scrubbing with chemical compounds. The work could also be dangerous, though at the time it wasn't clear quite how severe the effects could be. Since the days of Marie Curie (who died herself from something called "aplastic anaemia", due to exposure to radiation from her experiments), it had been known that radiation could cause serious illness.

After the war, hundreds of thousands of Japanese citizens were still suffering the after-effects of the radioactive atomic bombs dropped at Nagasaki and Hiroshima. Though Rosalind Franklin and her laboratory colleagues monitored the amount of radiation they were exposed to, the safety precautions taken were nothing like today.

Difficult Decisions

Rosalind wrote several times to her family that she was happy in Paris, despite the low pay and difficulties with rationing and transport strikes and accommodation. However, her parents especially were putting pressure on her to return. She did miss London, even with its smog-filled air. She had friends in Paris, but it was mostly a small circle of colleagues. Her siblings, and most of her friends, remained in England. The main reason she felt the pull of home, however, was the scientific community there and the employment prospects it offered.

A mind as restless as Rosalind's wouldn't allow her to tread water. If she stayed in France too long (she had already remained for over three years, having originally planned only two), she might find herself "locked out" for good. Getting a job in her narrow field relied on building a reputation. She could do that in France or in England but not both. In her letters to her mother and father, she reassured them she was coming home but not until she had found a job to go to.

One possibility was the Royal Institution, but she had already met the man who would be her boss there and she disliked him, calling him "odious" in a letter to her parents (but not naming him). Another option was Birkbeck College in Bloomsbury, London, where there was an esteemed research laboratory. John Desmond Bernal, who'd been head of crystallography at Cambridge when Rosalind was a student, had now moved to Birkbeck. Rosalind joined other ambitious scientists in applying for a job there.

She was rejected and put it down to the fact she still hadn't published many papers. She decided to remain in Paris a little longer, hoping her fortunes would change as more of her work found its way into scientific journals. Her boss at the Paris laboratory, Mering, learned of her plans to leave and took the news badly. Rosalind's ninth research paper, which appeared in the newly established journal, *Acta Crystallographica* in 1949, contained work they'd carried out together but he refused to allow his name to appear alongside hers. The rejection from a man she admired upset her a lot.

Still, it didn't hold Rosalind back for long.

She soon published a short paper in the British scientific journal, *Nature*. On the subject of coal and X-ray diffraction, Rosalind was becoming an internationally recognized name in her field.

After three years in Paris, while still looking for a job in England, Rosalind finally had enough of Madame Dumas and moved to a new apartment in the 7th *arrondissement*. She shared the apartment with two American scientists, a couple called Philip and Marion Hemily. Though it was further from her labs and more expensive, in other ways it was a more comfortable life: it had a telephone and a heated shower. However, it was sometimes awkward. Rosalind got on well with Philip, going on cycling trips with him, but not Marion. They often felt they were stepping on each other's toes and had little privacy. This unhappy arrangement further prompted Rosalind to speed up her job search in London.

Rosalind got in touch with a professor at King's College to ask about applying for a research fellowship and he told her that the best thing to do would be to contact the head of the department she wanted to work in. He was the first person to suggest that her work in investigating molecular structure could have uses in biological science, which wasn't a subject she'd studied since school.

In early 1950, she visited London and met up with John Turton Randall, the head of Biophysics at King's College, to apply for a fellowship. She had no great hopes of getting one, and it wasn't very clear exactly what she would be doing if she did, but she thought it was worth a shot. Randall was impressed by Rosalind's skillset and offered her a three-year position to study X-ray diffraction of proteins. She would be paid £750 a year, a good salary compared with other jobs she might have found within academia. It wasn't what she called a "particularly distinguished thing to apply for" but she said,

"...IF THE WORK AVAILABLE PLEASES ME, IT WOULD BE ALL RIGHT."

Rosalind's mixed feelings about leaving Paris come across in her letters. She talks about her "preference for Paris, the French way of life, the mass of French people and ... the Parisian climate", and her sadness at leaving people and places for good.

It was in Paris that she had spread her wings and made her reputation. It felt like she was clipping them again returning to a country where social boundaries and tradition were everywhere. She felt the English were more small-minded than the French. Even a couple of months before returning, Rosalind was still thinking about declining the job offer and staying where she was. She wrote that,

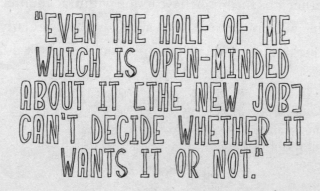

"EVEN THE HALF OF ME WHICH IS OPEN-MINDED ABOUT IT [THE NEW JOB] CAN'T DECIDE WHETHER IT WANTS IT OR NOT."

A Change of Focus

If she was unsure about King's College, she hid it from her future colleagues. She sent John Randall a long letter listing all the equipment she would need to get on with her work on arrival. His response was unexpected – he told her the assignment had changed somewhat. She would still be using X-ray diffraction, but not to look at proteins, but at "the structure of certain biological fibres". She would also be supervising a student called Ray Gosling (she was told it would just be the two of them working together). Randall felt the work might be more "profitable" or even "fundamental".

In many ways the focus of twentieth century science until that point had revolved around physics, from Einstein's theories at the start of the 1900s to the Manhattan Project that developed the first nuclear weapons during World War Two. The second half of the century began a biological revolution that we are still living through today.

These "fibres", as Randall called them, were strands of DNA, chains of a molecule found in the nucleus of almost all living cells. They were provided by a Swiss scientist called Rudolf Signer, who had extracted the DNA and prepared it in a special way that made analysis easier. Signer had displayed the DNA at a conference and then given samples to his audience, including Maurice Wilkins, Ray Gosling's previous supervisor at King's.

The change to Rosalind's work came as a surprise but not a particularly unwelcome one. DNA was long-thought to contain the mystery of genetic heredity – how offspring take on the physical characteristics of their parent organisms. She was excited about the opportunity to be part of a brand-new branch of science.

A Brief Word on Genetics

The work of the English scientist, Charles Darwin (1809–82), on evolution is considered an important foundation to genetics. After a long voyage on board an exploratory ship called HMS *Beagle*, on which he observed and collected many species of animal, he published his most famous work, *On the Origin of Species by Means of Natural Selection*, in 1859. His theory was that species did not remain the same over time but evolved. He believed that successful animals that were able to thrive, attract a mate and breed, passed on their successful traits to their young. And that with each generation, nature made small accidental changes to the genes of animals and these could be useful or not. If they were useful and those animals reproduced, the changes were passed on.

The theory suggested that all life on Earth evolved from one source, like the branches, twigs and stems all emerging from the same trunk of a tree. The most controversial part of his theory was the belief that we as humans are no different from all the other animals around us: we too evolved and shared a common ancestor with chimpanzees – at a fork in the branch, we developed into modern humans (*homo sapiens*) and they developed into chimpanzees (*pan troglodytes*).

RETURN TO LONDON

Home, Sweet Home?

I n January 1951, after four years in France, Rosalind started work at King's College. It proved to be a more difficult experience than she had expected.

London was still a mess after the German attacks in the war. The biophysics department was in a basement, right beside an enormous bomb crater. Rosalind was back living with her parents while she looked for somewhere to rent. After the independence of Paris, she found it stifling.

To her new colleagues, Rosalind came across as cold at first and even a little arrogant. Her upper-class accent stuck out when most of the students around her came from more humble backgrounds. Rosalind wasn't the sort of person who adjusted her personality to please other people but she couldn't help but feel like she didn't fit in anywhere in England.

Having experienced the lack of gender segregation in Paris, the rules at King's seemed even stricter. In London generally, there were many businesses that didn't employ women at all, like the bank where her father worked. Theology was the main subject taught at King's and the theologian student body and teaching staff were entirely male. Women were not even allowed in the senior common room where the male staff ate lunch. In her own biophysics department, the men socialized in nearby pubs and the women were not invited. It was so different from Rosalind's life in France. Though she found the arrangement irritating, she chose to focus on her work.

New Faces

She was introduced by John Randall, director of the Biophysics Department, to the people she would be working with: the doctoral student, Raymond (or Ray) Gosling, and a mathematician called Alex Stokes. When Rosalind started her job, the assistant director, Maurice Wilkins, was on holiday. It was Wilkins who'd been the one to convince Randall to change Rosalind's subject of study from proteins to DNA, though she did not know it at the time.

THE MYSTERY OF DNA

Scientists had known for some time what made up deoxyribonucleic acid (DNA). There were chemical compounds of sugars and phosphates, nitrogen-containing compounds called guanine, cytosine, adenine and thymine.

Chromosomes, which are packages of nucleic acid (DNA) molecules coiled tightly, had been observed in the nucleus of cells in the nineteenth century, but now scientists realized that there were sections of this DNA molecule called genes, which made proteins that told the body's cells to act in certain ways. However, how these molecules and compounds fitted together was still a mystery, as was how DNA copied itself.

In the preceding months, Gosling had managed to use X-ray crystallography to take very good quality images of the diffraction caused by DNA strands acquired from Rudolf Signer. The key was to hydrate (add water to) the samples, because they swelled and lengthened, making them easier to use. It seemed clear that DNA had a repeated, regular structure and Gosling had even speculated that DNA was structured in a helix pattern. Wilkins wanted Rosalind Franklin, who had a reputation for her crystallography, to work with Gosling and strengthen his team. Gosling was delighted at the prospect but Rosalind had no idea she was being brought in to work, effectively, on someone else's research. She'd thought, because of Randall's earlier letter to her, that it was only she and Gosling working on DNA.

She'd believed she'd be doing original research, independently, as she had been in Paris.

JT RANDALL

RAY GOSLING

It seems likely that Randall knew he had tricked Rosalind. Though he was known at the time for giving important roles to female scientists, he also knew how to persuade the best scientists to join his department. At the time, only one in a hundred Fellows of the Royal Society were women and it was still rare to find women in research roles. In any case, however much Randall respected Rosalind and the other members of his department, he probably didn't anticipate the huge

MAURICE WILKINS

row that would occur between Rosalind and Maurice Wilkins.

THE BIOPHYSICS DEPARTMENT AT KING'S COLLEGE

Rosalind ordered and assembled a new vacuum and camera equipment to make sure she'd be able to take the best images possible using X-ray diffraction. Wilkins returned in January 1951 and for a few months, they worked on separate projects, treating each other with polite respect.

Rosalind was also busy writing up a paper on coal, based on the work she'd done in Paris. Even though they weren't interacting much, there was still tension between the two and it isn't really clear why. They had the same academic interests, they both liked going to the theatre and had similar political views.

Maurice was perhaps keener to please others, while Rosalind had little time for that, particularly when she was busy working. There was also his unspoken superiority. He believed she was at the lab under his guidance and even if this wasn't said out loud, it might have affected his behaviour towards her. He certainly didn't realize the reputation she had from her previous work, or how senior and independent she had been in Paris. Coal was a mystery to him because it didn't relate to the field of biophysics at all. Their relationship was like a volcano, bubbling away and waiting to erupt.

There was some relief from the atmosphere at King's when Rosalind managed to move out of her parents' house to a new flat in South Kensington, further west. Here she cooked French cuisine for her friends and family, using garlic, which was an unusual ingredient in England at the time. She quickly made foreign friends at the lab and King's, but also became close to Gosling and his wife. The one person who was never invited to dinner was Maurice Wilkins.

Trouble in London

In May 1951, Wilkins gave a talk at a conference in Naples about the structure of DNA. He showed some of the images Gosling had taken at King's, the clearest to date, and the audience were impressed. One of those watching was Dr James Watson, originally from the University of Chicago but now doing research in Denmark. Watson was fascinated by genetics and nucleic acids and particularly the part about how DNA could be prepared prior to being bombarded with X-rays. This was key. In its naturally occurring state, in chromosomes, DNA is tightly coiled and irregularly shaped. Scientists had discovered it could be stretched out and fixed in position – imagine uncurling a tightly coiled snake.

Other scientists had proposed helix-shaped models of DNA for the past fifteen years but Rosalind wasn't one for building models unless she could actually see the helix through her own diffraction images. Rosalind was not a theorist but an experimenter and a crystallographer. She was interested in creating models from her images, not models from theories. Her love of the practical side of science can be traced back to her schooldays at St Paul's, when she and her fellow students were encouraged to be very careful with their practical experiments, moving in slow and steady steps through their work.

And so, in the basement at King's, Rosalind busied herself with putting together the new X-ray equipment alongside Ray Gosling. One of the main difficulties in acquiring good images via X-ray diffraction was controlling the levels of moisture in the camera. Humidity made the DNA sample being analysed expand further, but she found she could extract the moisture as well, re-shrinking the DNA to its dry form. With varying levels of hydration, the DNA sample could be analysed in a variety of states and reused several times.

The precision of these techniques was new to Wilkins. He was impressed and a little bit left out. Rosalind thought that there was little point in him being there if he couldn't offer useful advice on the work they were doing! He was nothing like her brilliant mentor in Paris,

Jacques Mering, whom she'd admired a lot.

Wilkins was keen to mend the troubled relationship. The problem was that Rosalind, engaged in her work, had no interest in doing so. At one point, he bought her a box of chocolates – but it was a foolish gesture. Rosalind wasn't someone who could be charmed by a silly gift and she knew that Wilkins would never have bought sweets for a male colleague. They were very much opposites – he, shy and slow to speak his mind, Rosalind, quite sure in her opinions and not afraid to express them. She was used to arguing with men and being treated as an equal but Maurice behaved sulkily and they both said unkind things behind each other's backs.

THE RACE TO DNA

King's College wasn't the only scientific institution looking at the structure and workings of organic molecules. At Cavendish Laboratory in Cambridge, Lawrence Bragg (whose lectures Rosalind had attended while at Newnham College) was studying proteins using crystallography, alongside a young British molecular biologist called Francis Crick. At the California Institute of Technology, or "Caltech", the biochemist Linus Pauling published important discoveries on the structure of proteins too – work that would later win him a Nobel Prize. Pauling, hearing about the work in Europe, was ready to move on to DNA himself. The other person in the conversation was John Bernal, at Birkbeck College, London,

LINUS PAULING

whom Rosalind had applied to work for. Rosalind was impressed with his attitude to scientific investigation, which lined up with her own. Bernal wanted to use X-ray diffraction to prove how DNA was structured, not to make guesses based on incomplete science.

The various efforts to understand DNA made it a race but that didn't mean there was no teamwork along the way. Each of the labs had slightly different expertise and shared information when it helped them – after all, there were only a few people in the world with the knowledge and the facilities to carry out these complex experiments. They met at conferences, published their findings in the same journals and occasionally visited each other's laboratories. But there was still an edge of competition and findings weren't always shared immediately. No one wanted to get things wrong in front of their rivals or help someone else get to the answer first.

Rosalind's pictures were already making waves. It was at Cambridge's Cavendish Laboratory that Maurice Wilkins told a gathering of other scientists about their DNA findings at King's.

He said that the images Gosling and Rosalind had produced suggested strongly that DNA was shaped in a helix structure. His claim angered Rosalind – perhaps because she felt he was interpreting her images but also because Wilkins wasn't an expert in the field. Rosalind felt that Wilkins was jumping to conclusions and that while DNA was sometimes a helix when it was artificially hydrated, the images weren't good enough to confirm that DNA was always a helix in its naturally occurring, "dry" state.

The images Wilkins and Stokes based their theory on looked like a fuzzy X shape. Rosalind realized that one of the reasons for the imperfect images was that the hydration of the samples varied. If the moisture levels changed in the middle of the imaging process (which could take several days), the image would be blurred and hard to interpret. She called the un-hydrated form of DNA, "dry", or the "A-form". The hydrated, longer fibres were called the "wet", or "B-form". With the latter, she got increasingly clear pictures.

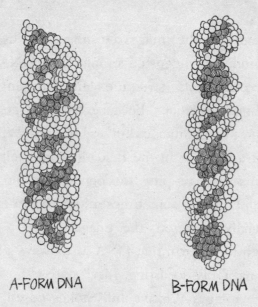

A-FORM DNA   B-FORM DNA

This isn't a picture of DNA itself but shows how the X-rays passing through the DNA molecules are bent around before hitting a photographic plate. Many factors affect the quality of the image but the main ones are the size and purity of the DNA sample, the hydration levels, the quality of the vacuum in the tube, the precision of the camera and the angle at which the X-ray beam is fired at the sample. As in a normal photograph, keeping everything perfectly still is crucial. Rosalind was a specialist in all these factors; Maurice Wilkins was not. After he had given his speech to their peers, she confronted him and told him to, "Go back to your microscopes." She meant that he shouldn't interfere with her X-ray work. Their conflict had finally come to a head and it was Rosalind who snapped first.

She took a holiday in France with friends to get away from the lab. News of the trouble spread through the DNA community. At Caltech, Linus Pauling asked Randall to send him copies of the photos from Wilkins's lab and Randall refused. Everyone seemed aware that they were on the verge of some big discovery. Scorned by Rosalind, Wilkins turned to Francis Crick at the Cavendish lab. He asked Alex Stokes, the mathematician at King's, to calculate exactly what the X-ray diffraction pattern would look like if A-form DNA was a helix. It turned out to be an X-shape, very similar to the images they were getting. It was enough for Wilkins to write to Crick with a sketched diagram of how DNA might be structured. Wilkins, about to go off to a conference, left a note for Rosalind explaining the work he and Stokes had been doing. He asked her to investigate. This method of working backwards was exactly the sort of thing Rosalind hated and she resented his attempts to direct her work. When she returned from holiday and found his note, she felt unhappy.

She and Gosling were perfecting their X-ray techniques, working long and painstaking hours. When Wilkins came back from his conference, refreshed and optimistic, he was amazed by Rosalind's images, which closely resembled more and more the theoretical drawings Stokes had made. He asked Rosalind if she would like to collaborate with him and Stokes on analysing some DNA samples he'd obtained in the United States. If he was trying to hold out an olive branch, it didn't have the desired affect. Rosalind erupted in fury. She claimed he was trying to interpret her data for her and treading on her toes. In her mind, she'd achieved the images through her own hard work and Wilkins was trying to use his position as assistant director of the lab to claim some form of ownership. Rosalind wasn't interested in the same race as Wilkins – she only wanted to be allowed to do her own work, forming her own conclusions, in her own time. The breakdown of their relationship was complete and Rosalind wrote to her friend Adrienne Weill in despair that the lab was going through "the blackest of crises" and she wanted "to get out as soon as possible". She was even considering returning to Paris.

John Randall and Ray Gosling were caught between the warring pair. Randall called them into his office, like a headteacher summoning two naughty pupils, and decided that they should work separately from then on. Wilkins could take his DNA samples from the States, supplied by Columbia University (this was B-form, wet DNA) and Rosalind could continue to use the Signer A-form, dry DNA. This was the better option for Rosalind, because of the careful way Signer had prepared the samples.

The new arrangement suited Rosalind not only because she had more promising DNA to work with but because she was free of Wilkins looking over her shoulder. He, on the other hand, struggled to work alone and began spending more time visiting Francis Crick in Cambridge. James Watson, previously at Copenhagen, had also arrived at Cavendish Laboratory, eager to continue his investigations into the gene. The pieces were moving into position for what would be the discovery of the century.

Francis Crick and James Watson got on from the start. Watson's life had been spent in biology and genetics; Crick's in physics and crystallography. For the new science of biophysics, they were a perfect team. But they both worked under Lawrence Bragg and he wanted Crick to maintain focus on proteins. For now, their hands were tied.

Because Wilkins knew this, he felt he didn't need to conceal the work he was doing in Randall's lab at King's. On his many visits to Cambridge, he told Crick and Watson everything and whinged a good deal about Rosalind, whom he called Rosy – a nickname she hated. They wanted him and Rosalind to build a model of DNA, as others were attempting but Wilkins knew Rosalind's feelings about models and didn't press her.

Models and Mistakes

In November 1951, King's College held a meeting to discuss the structure of DNA.

Wilkins and Rosalind both spoke to the audience, as well as Gosling. Most of the attendees knew about the disagreements going on in the King's lab. Watson was among them and in his later memoir, *The Double Helix*, he seems to concentrate more on what Rosalind was wearing rather than what she said. He wondered, in sexist language, "How she would look if she took off her glasses and did something novel with her hair."

If he had been focusing on the content of her speech, he might have learned something important. Scientists knew what DNA was made up of but the precise structure was still a mystery. Rosalind's knowledge of chemistry and work with hydrated DNA samples led her to suppose that the phosphates could not be on the inside of the chain, as Watson and Crick supposed, but on the outside.

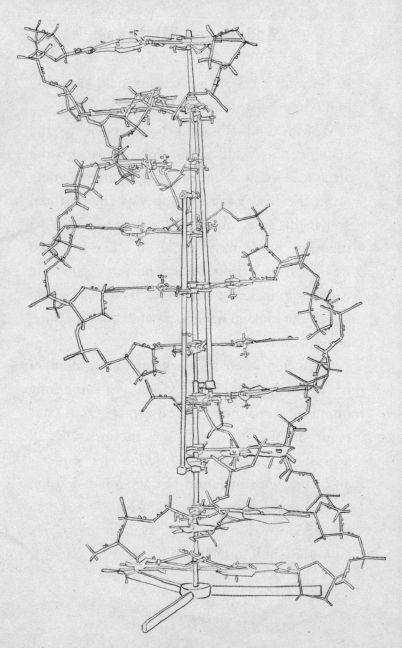

Crick and Watson were building a model of their own and showed it to Rosalind when she visited the Cavendish lab in Cambridge. Rosalind immediately told them that it was wrong. Watson found her manner aggressive but that may just have been his wounded pride. For Rosalind, it proved her belief that model-building was pointless without sound experimental data. Bragg, who was in charge of Crick and Watson, saw Rosalind was correct in her assessment. Frustrated with the mistakes Crick and Watson were making, he ordered them to stop working on DNA. For now, King's was back in the lead of the pack.

FRANCIS CRICK   JAMES WATSON

Wanted: A New Job

Rosalind went back to Paris to visit some old colleagues. She didn't tell the King's lab that she was going to see if she could get her old job back. She met her former neighbour, Vittorio Luzzati, who told her about a new way to analyse diffraction images called the Patterson Function. It involved taking a number of images by tilting the X-ray camera at different angles, then using extremely complicated mathematics to compare the results. By doing so, a 3D model of the sample could be worked out.

While in Paris, Rosalind was delighted to meet with her old mentor Adrienne Weill but seeing Jacques Mering again was unpleasant. He had still not forgiven her for abandoning his lab for London and made it clear there would be no job in the city she loved. In her letters to Anne Sayre at the time, Rosalind sounded deeply unhappy, criticising her King's colleagues ("the middle and senior people are positively repulsive" and "there isn't a first-class or even a good brain among them"). She longed to work among old colleagues again, as she felt like an outsider in England. She wrote,

"I SUSPECT THAT I ENJOYED BEING A MORE INTERESTING PERSON IN FRANCE THAN I AM IN ENGLAND."

Despairing at the thought of being stuck at King's, Rosalind met with John Bernal at Birkbeck in secret and asked to join his department. He gave her no concrete offer but said he would be happy to have her in future. She returned to King's unhappily, where Wilkins especially described her as looking miserable and reacting angrily to even the smallest irritation. ("Franklin barks often," he wrote, "but doesn't often succeed in biting me.") There are also records of her kindness too, especially to the younger students of King's. As ever, she got on well with Ray Gosling and the mathematician Alex Stokes. She was always happy to explain her work and encourage others – what she couldn't stand was anyone interfering.

Rosalind put the Patterson technique into

practice, spending long hours with Gosling, setting up the camera and carrying out the calculations. On 7 February, 1952, she submitted a report in which she detailed the process and findings of the last few months. Though she didn't build a model, she suggested the DNA molecule was possibly a helix-shaped structure of two, three or four chains, with the backbone rungs of phosphates on the outside. Around a week later, Francis Crick submitted a paper to *Acta Crystallographica* in which he predicted the X-ray diffraction pattern from atoms organized in a helix. All the teams in the race were closing in on the finish line.

Photograph 51

After a walking holiday in Wales with a friend from Paris, Rosalind attended another conference in London, this one organized by the Royal Society. The guest of honour was Robert Corey, a colleague of Linus Pauling, from Caltech. She showed some of her photographs to Corey, who reported home that they were excellent.

James Watson was also in attendance at the

conference. Though he was no longer officially working on DNA, he still hadn't forgotten his quest to understand its structure. He wrote to a colleague that "the people at King's are involved in a fight among themselves" and if they "persist in doing nothing, we shall again try our luck".

While Rosalind was at the conference, Gosling was managing the apparatus at King's, taking yet another exposure of DNA. Though they were supposed to be working with the dry A-form, sometimes moisture levels in the tube would alter it to the lengthened B-form. This happened during the taking of the famous "Photograph 51" – and when Rosalind returned to the lab on 2 May, she saw the best image yet of the B-form of DNA – a clear X shape, with striped dark and light arms. It matched perfectly with Stokes's calculations and showed once and for all that the B-form of DNA was a helix. Rosalind, who had strongly believed this to be the case anyway, put the image aside.

In her mind, she was meant to be studying the A-form of the nucleic acid and just because it was a helix when hydrated, didn't mean it would be helical when dry. Her photographs of the A-form were much fuzzier and more indistinct. Rosalind wasn't saying the A-form wasn't a helix, only that her evidence didn't lead to that conclusion. Like any careful experimental scientist, she wasn't willing to engage in wishful thinking. Francis Crick, and other supporters of the helix structure, thought she was close-minded and that she was interpreting her measurements incorrectly. Rosalind wasn't close-minded but she was cautious. If Rosalind had had the time to continue with her research, she no doubt would have confirmed that A-form samples showed a helix as well. She saw no need to rush and returned to her work. Photograph 51 remained in a drawer, unseen by anyone except Rosalind and Gosling.

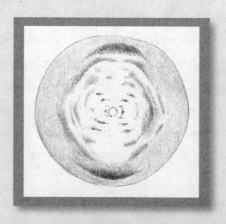

MYSTERY SOLVED

In spring 1952, J D Bernal at Birkbeck offered Rosalind a role in his lab, as long as her current boss, Randall, agreed. It appears he did so readily. Some have speculated that it was Randall himself who convinced Bernal to take Rosalind on. In whatever case, he was probably pleased to let her go and get her out of King's, as it was clear that Maurice Wilkins and Rosalind were never going to get on.

Wilkins had mixed feelings about Rosalind leaving. He was disappointed that things hadn't worked out but also relieved that he could resume his work on the A-form DNA, which Rosalind had been using exclusively. And he still had Ray Gosling to help him. For her part, Rosalind was now free (although she wasn't leaving King's until the end of the year), she made a rare joke, writing a "death notice" for Wilkins. (In Victorian times and later, death notices were postcards sent when a person died. They typically had a black border.) It read:

"It is with great regret that we have to announce the death, on Friday 18 July 1952, of DNA helix (crystalline). Death followed a protracted illness. A memorial service will be held next Monday or Tuesday. It is hoped that Dr M H F Wilkins will speak in memory of the late helix."

It was signed by Rosalind and Ray Gosling. Alex Stokes later said that Wilkins did not find it funny and his pride was wounded.

Meanwhile, at the other competing labs, the contenders were making progress. By Christmas of 1952, Crick and Watson heard that Linus Pauling at Caltech had worked out the structure of DNA and would be making a model and publishing his findings. The news hit Watson especially hard. He told Maurice Wilkins, who suggested all was not lost. He would soon have access to Rosalind's A-form Signer DNA and they'd be able make a new model themselves. The race wasn't over until papers were published.

A Fresh Start

At the start of 1953, Rosalind was finalizing her work at King's in preparation for her move to Birkbeck in March. She would have left earlier but a bout of flu had kept her away from the labs for several weeks, so she was behind schedule. Still, she was getting good results from her diffractions and found it hard to stop work. She also had three papers to finish and submit on the investigations and findings on both forms of DNA. She'd heard of Pauling and Corey's discovery, too, but didn't know the details. Everyone at Birkbeck, the Cavendish lab and King's was waiting for a draft copy of the Pauling paper.

At the same time, Gosling was trying to work out his place at King's. He'd enjoyed his work with Rosalind and respected her a great deal but now he would have to continue under his former supervisor, Wilkins. In preparation for the switch, he showed Wilkins Photograph 51 – there was no reason not to.

When Linus Pauling's draft paper on DNA

arrived, in late January, Watson could hardly contain his delight when he saw the conclusions were undoubtedly wrong. In fact, it resembled the same model he and Crick had made at the Cavendish – the one Rosalind had criticized. But the Pauling paper had been accepted for publication in February's *Proceedings of the National Academy of Sciences*. As soon as Pauling's error was discovered, Watson would begin work again. They didn't have long.

On 30 January, James Watson turned up at Rosalind's lab uninvited and asked if she wanted to see the mistakes in the Pauling paper, which he'd brought with him. The pair argued, with Watson insisting that the A-form of DNA was helix-shaped. According to Watson, Rosalind became very angry. He wrote later: "Suddenly Rosy came from behind the lab bench that separated us and began moving towards me. Fearing that in her hot anger she might strike me, I grabbed up the Pauling manuscript and hastily retreated to the open door."

We only have Watson's account, so whether the explosion of fury was as bad as he suggests is hard to say. In any case, she had a right to be angry on this occasion. Rosalind's lab space was sacred to her and Watson was invading it. He wasn't even employed at King's!

On his retreat from her lab, Watson ran into Wilkins. After sympathizing with the intruder about Rosalind's behaviour, Wilkins showed him Photograph 51. Watson realized its importance at once, writing in his memoir that "my mouth fell open and my pulse began to race". Wilkins didn't fully understand the importance – he just thought it was a particularly clear image. At her speech for the King's College meeting in November 1951, Rosalind had explained her theories about the helix structure of B-form DNA. All the photo did was confirm what she had already said.

But Watson knew the image was something very special indeed. He returned to Cambridge that night with the secret of life at his fingertips and with the clear idea DNA was a double helix made up of phosphates and sugars on the outside strands, joined by base pairs of adenine and cytosine, guanine and thymine on the inside.

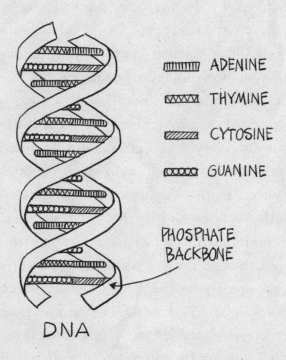

ADENINE

THYMINE

CYTOSINE

GUANINE

PHOSPHATE
BACKBONE

DNA

Watson and Crick got to work ordering the parts for a model the very next day. They knew they had a headstart on Pauling and the King's lab. Bragg, the director of the Cavendish, approved their new enterprise for the prestige it would bring. They worked through early February and, when Wilkins came to visit, they asked his permission to build a model based on

Photograph 51 (in fact the process was already well underway). Wilkins left the meeting with the feeling he might have given away too much. Crucially, he hadn't asked Rosalind's permission to share her image.

And that wasn't the only way Rosalind helped Crick and Watson. The previous December, she had written a report of her DNA findings for the Medical Research Council (MRC) which provided funding to King's College. One of the members of the MRC committee happened to be Max Perutz, who was also connected with Bragg's Cavendish lab. He shared it with Crick and Watson.

The final stage of the puzzle was working out how the four bases – adenine (A), thymine (T), guanine (G) and cytosine (C) – fit together inside the phosphate chains like the rungs of a ladder. Each of these molecules has a certain size and shape based on they way their atoms are structured. It was known that there were the same number of A and T and the same number of G and C (these were called "Chargaff ratios", after the scientist who discovered them). Rosalind thought that perhaps adenine and thymine were interchangeable, as were guanine and cytosine. She was close, but not quite there.

The Finish Line

It was Watson who realized the truth and his models helped him to see it. He understood that when adenine joined to thymine, the combined bases formed the same molecular shape as when guanine joined to cytosine. This made sense of the Chargaff ratios: G always combined with C and A always joined with T; that's why there were the same number of each.

It seems simple and in some ways it is. It also explains (very basically) how DNA copies itself exactly. When it's ready to replicate, the "ladder" splits down the middle. The base pairs break apart. We now understand that enzymes (protein molecules that speed up a reaction in an organism) rebuild the missing side of the strand, connecting a new C to every G and a new A to every T in this way, the new strand is a perfect replica of the broken one.

As Watson and Crick were coming to their conclusions at the Cavendish, Maurice Wilkins was looking forward to Rosalind's departure from King's College. He wrote to Crick on 7 March, "Our dark lady leaves us next week... At last the decks are clear and we can put all hands to the pumps." By referring to "us" and "we", he seems unaware of just how far Crick and Watson had already ventured. It was the same day that they finalized their model.

It's easy to overstate the importance of Photograph 51. Certainly the image was the clearest yet and it had quite an impression on James Watson. It was a flash of brilliant light in the darkness. But James Watson was still the one who deduced DNA structure from the image – he made the leap of understanding. Though the data was handed to him on a plate, few people could have interpreted it. Others, including Rosalind herself, had seen the same data without the same revelation.

It seems fair to say that others would have come to the same conclusions about DNA's structure and soon, if Watson had not got there first. In fact, in the same week as Crick and Watson were reading her report, Rosalind made some calculations based on another of her images, Photograph 49, and made a note that it could show a "two-chain helix". And by 23 February, she'd also analysed Photograph 51 and was having similar ideas to Watson – that the A-form of DNA was a two-chain helix as well.

But she had two papers to finish, so she put the DNA work aside.

The Secret is Out

When Maurice Wilkins found out about Crick and Watson's model, he concealed any annoyance at being kept in the dark and congratulated them. When he told Rosalind, she didn't seem to care a great deal either. She still had several papers in the pipeline and she was thinking about the future under John Bernal at Birkbeck. It's not clear if Rosalind knew that her photograph and her report had been seen by the Cavendish duo, though she must have been able to make an educated guess at what had happened.

For John Randall it was quite a different story. He was incredibly disappointed that Cambridge had beaten the King's team. Crick and Watson were in a difficult position. They wanted to submit a paper to *Nature*, detailing the discovery but it would be impossible to explain how they'd reached their conclusions without referring to Rosalind's work. After all, the whole of the experimental data crucial to their findings came from Wilkins's lab, and from Rosalind Franklin particularly. Negotiations between Wilkins, Randall and the Cavendish team began, and it was decided that three papers would be submitted to *Nature*, the lead one from Crick and Watson and two support papers from King's; one by Wilkins, and the other under Rosalind and Gosling's names. The combined papers would give a picture of the labs working on the same problems, if not together, then in a spirit of sharing information. The editors at *Nature* had no idea of the truth when they published the three papers on the 25 April 1953.

Before her own paper went to print, which

included Photograph 51, Rosalind inserted a note,

"THUS OUR GENERAL IDEAS ARE CONSISTENT WITH THE MODEL PROPOSED BY CRICK AND WATSON."

This was despite the fact that it was actually Crick and Watson's model that was derived from her data. If she was aware of how backwards the statement was, perhaps she was being sarcastic.

Aftermath

The effect of the *Nature* papers was not as earth-shattering as Crick and Watson had hoped. Though Rosalind's experimental data supported their conclusions, it wasn't proof. Perhaps this explains why she wasn't more annoyed at her work being used – to her meticulous eye, they hadn't solved the problem yet but were only moving in the right direction. She still referred to Crick and Watson's work as merely a "model" rather than the actual structure of DNA. And no one yet knew exactly how DNA separated or how it bonded together again.

When Rosalind moved to Birkbeck, Randall, perhaps still upset from losing the race, asked her to stop studying DNA. He suggested it wouldn't be right, now she was no longer part of his lab. Rosalind ignored him and continued to communicate with Ray Gosling on their nucleic acid work. Gosling offered his heartfelt and sincere thanks to her in the acknowledgements when he published his doctoral thesis later in 1953.

Birkbeck was very different to King's. The labs weren't purpose built but instead could be found in a row of converted, bomb-damaged residential buildings on Torrington Square. Her own lab was on the fifth floor, under a leaky roof. But it was Bernal who'd brought her there, not the facilities. He was a world-renowned figure in physics and crystallography and a fellow of the Royal Society. Charismatic, highly intelligent and an efficient fundraiser for his department, he was as close to a celebrity as a scientist could be. He attracted talent and money from far and wide. He was happy for Rosalind to finish up her DNA work before embarking on something new. To show there were no hard feelings, she continued to correspond with Francis Crick on the finer points of the nucleic acid molecule. Over the following years, the two became respectful collaborators and close friends.

Before she began properly at Birkbeck, Rosalind took a long holiday to Israel, a country she'd never visited before. Israel had only been an independent state for five years, established after World War Two as a homeland for the persecuted Jewish population of Europe. She had mixed feelings about the visit. Though she enjoyed the weather, visiting the historical sites and meeting students at the Weizmann Institute of Science, the more traditional Jewish community made her feel uncomfortable. For someone who mixed with people of all different backgrounds and religions and political ideas, she thought the strict customs of dress and worship stifling, especially to children.

BIRKBECK AND VIRUSES

Rosalind's new area of research at Birkbeck was to be the tobacco mosaic virus (TMV).

WHAT IS A VIRUS?

A virus is a nucleic acid molecule wrapped in a protein shell that infects a cell and replicates itself like a parasite. It is basically a copying mechanism that hijacks a cell and uses its resources, before spreading elsewhere (called contagion). Viruses exist everywhere in nature and can infect all living things, plant or animal, and many are species specific. In humans, we are familiar with those that carry diseases like the common cold or chicken pox.

The tobacco mosaic virus (TMV) was the first virus to be identified by scientists in the 1890s. It damages tobacco crops, mottling the leaves with a distinct pattern. TMV was also the first virus to be isolated and crystallized (that is, preserved in a solid, regular form), making it a perfect sample for crystallography. Bernal himself had done pioneering work, and a year earlier, James Watson had used crystallography to show that units of protein were wrapped around a nucleic acid helix – however, this one wasn't comprised of DNA but RNA.

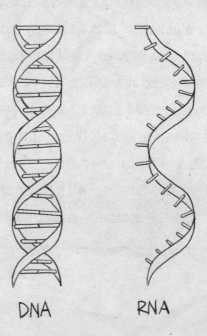

DNA   RNA

RNA

RNA, or ribonucleic acid, is present in all living cells. Its principal role is to act as a messenger carrying instructions from DNA for making proteins. In viruses, it carries the instructions to help with the copying process. Whereas DNA consists of two strands of phosphates joined by two bases, RNA is a single spiral strand, with single bases attached.

Rosalind realized the work was going to be more complex than her investigations at King's but she was looking forward to it. She was already getting the first promising images, when she received an unexpected invitation from the other side of the Atlantic.

A Visit to the States

Until this point in her life, Rosalind Franklin had needed to chase all her professional opportunities.

But now one came calling for her. Her work on DNA was still not widely known outside a small circle (whereas Crick and Watson were almost celebrities, featured in mainstream magazines like *Vogue*), but the papers she'd published on coal following her time at BCURA and in Paris had made a real impact. She was invited by the American Association for the Advancement of Science to attend a conference about coal in New Hampshire.

But she'd need money to get there. Rosalind wrote to several universities and laboratories, offering to give lectures in return for their sponsorship. Eventually, she secured a visa and set off.

James Watson was now living and working at Caltech and offered his help by introducing her to Nobel Laureate, Wendell Stanley, who ran the new Virus Laboratory at the University of Berkeley, California. Stanley offered some of her expenses in return for lecturing, as did Linus Pauling at Caltech. Her reputation helped a great deal.

At first she was refused a visa by the American

Embassy because they were wary about letting in people who could potentially take American jobs. Help came from the US Bureau of Mines and the National Carbon Research Laboratories in Cleveland, as both vouched for her to appeal the decision. Rosalind promised that she wouldn't actually be earning any money on the trip and would pay back any money received minus her travel and living expenses.

When the time for the trip came, Rosalind had a full schedule planned, criss-crossing the country. The flight there was a daunting prospect. Though she'd flown between London and Paris several times, this journey consisted of several parts; stopping to refuel in Scotland, Iceland, Newfoundland, and then Nova Scotia. Due to various delays, she arrived eleven hours late!

She carried out her duties in New Hampshire, delivering a lecture on coal, before moving on to the Massachusetts Institute of Technology (MIT) in Boston, then the Marine Biological Laboratory at Woods Hole, Cape Cod, where she experienced her first hurricane, which lifted boats from the sea and flung them on to land. Rosalind liked Boston, particularly the beautiful, spacious buildings and the brilliant sunshine. She also enjoyed the open-mindedness of the scientific community and the facilities available. She was less impressed with the huge food portion sizes though, writing "they have everything and too much of it" and criticizing the lack of skill in cooking, implying it was tasteless.

In New York City, Rosalind was astounded by the towering buildings but she thought New Yorkers could be "rude". Her trip continued, first in Philadelphia, where her old friend Anne Sayre now lived, then inland to Pittsburgh, Cleveland, Chicago, St Louis and Madison, Wisconsin. Along the way, she met many of the scientists she knew by name, towering figures in genetics and crystallography such as Erwin Chargaff and Isidor Fankuchen. She also gave her coal lecture at a number of scientific institutions. It was a trip of two sides. On the one hand, she was a much-respected authority on coal but when she entered biology labs, she realized she was very much a novice.

After a sightseeing trip to the Grand Canyon, she finally reached the West Coast, visiting the University of California at Los Angeles (UCLA) and then Caltech, where she gave talks on her latest TMV work, attended by Linus Pauling himself. She also met James Watson once more, who told her about advances in TMV analysis being done by a crystallographer at Yale called Don Caspar. Rosalind wasn't as fond of the West Coast as the East. Watson drove her to LA and Hollywood, which she found "characterless". Finally, she visited San Francisco for five days and the Virus Laboratory of Wendell, which she found "unfriendly".

DONALD CASPAR

She was glad to fly back to Washington DC for a brief stay with a scientist called Alexander Rich and his wife. Rich was also doing work on TMV and showed her around the city. Overall, her impression of the United States was positive. Certainly for someone who loved the outdoors, the scale of the scenery and nature made her warm to the place. She described the weather, aside from the hurricanes, as "heavenly". There was little of the English formality in America and much less sexism in the sciences and in the way men and woman worked together. It looked very much like a land of opportunity. She told her parents in a letter,

"THE UNIVERSITY SCIENTISTS ARE AS FINE A CROWD AS I'VE MET ANYWHERE."

She surely had her own unhappy experiences in mind when she added,

"THEY SEEM VERY GOOD AT WORKING TOGETHER HAPPILY AND UNSELFISHLY IN GROUPS IN A WAY THAT IS RARE IN ENGLAND."

Rosalind left New York on the French transatlantic liner, *Liberté*, ready to take advantage of those opportunities. She'd made contacts at the forefront of her field from across the United States and, though still new to the world of viruses, she would soon make her mark.

A New Team

Rosalind wasn't working alone at Birkbeck. Before she'd even travelled to America, she met a South African scientist called Aaron Klug, at the time working in the same building as her on Torrington Square. A crystallographer too, when he saw her initial diffraction images of the tobacco mosaic virus, he was hooked. As he said later, "my fate was sealed". John Bernal agreed he could switch to studying TMV, in collaboration with Rosalind. From the start they were

AARON KLUG

NORMAN PIRIE

an excellent team, he a theorist and she a brilliant experimenter. Rosalind needed moral support in her work because she had made a new enemy in the ranks of virus research, a British virologist called Norman W Pirie. He was renowned for a paper which specified the long, thin shape of the virus – like a rod.

Rosalind submitted a new paper to *Nature*, in which she spelled out more accurately the structure of TMV, based on her images and calculation. One of her findings was that TMV rods were always the same length.

Pirie saw the manuscript of the paper before it was published and disagreed, writing a strongly worded letter to Rosalind criticizing her methods and findings. His tone was condescending and he insisted on listing what he saw as her faults.

Rosalind defended herself – the data supported her view. The paper was published as planned and Pirie never forgave her for not heeding his criticisms. It turned out Rosalind was correct and

Pirie was wrong. The first stage of his revenge was petty – he refused to send her any further samples of TMV from his stock. But there was worse to come because Pirie wasn't only well-known, but influential too.

Still, Rosalind and Klug continued their research by sourcing the virus elsewhere and growing their own. Rosalind published another paper in *Nature* a few months later, in 1955. Two admirers were Francis Crick and James Watson, now based at separate labs, also working on RNA and the TMV virus at the same time as Rosalind. Only on this occasion, the spirit of cooperation was real.

Rosalind was not officially a member of the staff at Birkbeck – she had no set teaching duties. Her pay came as a three-year grant offered by the Agricultural Research Council (ARC) and she had the freedom to choose whom she worked with. First, she and Klug took on two doctoral students and in the summer of 1955 a fifth member joined the team. Don Caspar, who Watson had mentioned to Rosalind on her American visit, held a PhD in molecular biology.

His work on TMV fit well with hers and they became close colleagues. He'd discovered that the virus "rod" was hollow, which came as a surprise, because people had thought the virus's RNA filled its centre. Rosalind uncovered the answer based on her own images – the nucleic acid strands were coiled between nobbly protein units called "capsomeres" that stuck out from the outside of the virus. The whole thing looked a bit like a cob of corn with the central cylinder scooped out. This provided a clue as to how the virus actually worked.

Remember that a virus infects a cell. The protein shell helps protect the nucleic acid while the virus gets inside the new cell. Then it sheds off and the nucleic acid is free to copy itself.

Rosalind's group moved on to a variety of plant viruses, including turnips, potatoes, tomatoes and cucumbers, with excellent results. Not all were rod-shaped, like TMV – some were spherical.

But trouble was brewing in the form of her new enemy, Norman Pirie. It seemed he'd protested against Rosalind's work and used his influence to prevent the ARC from giving her funding.

As always when she faced difficulties, Rosalind concentrated on getting her work done. And unlike at King's, when she'd been junior and isolated, she now had lots of contacts, both in the United States and Europe, who were happy to send her equipment and samples. She was determined to keep Aaron Klug at her side and forcefully continued to make her case for more secure funding. She awaited their response. Her work, she knew, was important. As she wrote to the ARC's secretary, William Slater, it would answer "what is probably the most fundamental of all questions about the mechanism of living processes".

Though her team was precarious, her laboratory was at the forefront of research. Rosalind began to produce a series of influential papers on viruses throughout 1955 and 1956. She attended and spoke at conferences across London, in front of familiar faces such as Mering and Pauling. Afterwards, many of the same crowd attended a crystallography symposium in Madrid and Rosalind took a week's holiday in the country afterwards with Francis Crick and his wife, Odile.

On her return to England, there was good news. The American conference that she'd attended two years before wanted her to come back and the topic wasn't coal this time but nucleic acids. She got permission to stall her work at Birkbeck for two months in order to take part in the conference.

Whereas funding for the journey to America had been hard to source in 1954, there were no such struggles now. She was a rising star, with a global reputation in her field. The Rockefeller foundation offered to pay both for her trip to the conference and a tour of the country and its main laboratories afterwards.

She flew to New York in May and this time the visit was more leisurely. As well as New Hampshire, she visited Baltimore, Cape Cod and California. There was more time to enjoy herself outside of scientific discussions, in the pursuits she'd always loved. She swam in the sea and lakes and went for long hikes, camping overnight. There was one scary moment when she was sailing with a friend on a lake near the city of Madison, Wisconsin and a storm blew up, driving them back to shore under thunderous rain. But for the most part the trip wasn't dangerous. On the West Coast, she sunbathed and she climbed mountains in the Sierra Nevada. She wrote to her sister that she "completely fell for Southern California".

America suited Rosalind well and offered an enticing possibility. Tired of relying on ARC and William Slater for approval on her equipment and team, she was told there might be another way to secure funds for her work, by applying to the US National Institutes of Health in Washington. If she did so, she really would be entering the leagues of the global scientists – people like Crick and Watson, who hopped across the Atlantic frequently, working with the best and brightest and dispensing their wisdom like stardust to labs across the Western world. Charmed by the United States and all it had to offer, the future looked very bright indeed.

CLOUDS IN A BLUE SKY

Rosalind had been unwell throughout her childhood and even as an adult there had been minor illnesses that caused her to miss work for a few weeks at a time. While she was still in California, she began to suffer stomach pains but wasn't overly concerned. After visiting an American doctor, she was prescribed painkillers and the symptoms went away.

The next stage of her trip was a three-week stint at Wendell's Virus Laboratory at Berkeley. As with her last trip to the States, it was the lowlight of her visit. She thought the people there took "themselves far too seriously" and weren't that friendly. It may have also been that her mood was low because she'd received bad news from her American friend and colleague, Don Caspar. His father had died in his home city of Colorado Springs, so Caspar wouldn't be coming to meet her as planned.

The couple Rosalind was staying with in Berkeley, the geneticists, Erwin and Ethel Tessman, felt sorry for her and decided to help her get to see Caspar anyway, even though it was around 1,900 kilometres from the Californian coast to Colorado Springs in Denver. Rosalind hitched a ride with their friend to Salt Lake City, a trip that took over two days, through the desert and over the Rocky Mountains. She then flew the rest of the way to see her friend.

Though nobody will ever know for sure, it's possible that Rosalind had fallen in love with Caspar. Caspar was unmarried but younger than Rosalind and she may have been wary of crossing a boundary with him. She left after a short visit and spent a weekend in Cape Cod before heading to New York for the final stage of her American trip. It was here that her abdominal pains returned and she found she could no longer zip her skirt over the bulge in her stomach.

Back in London on 24 August, she went to see her doctor in Hampstead. Having ruled out pregnancy, she sent Rosalind to another doctor at University College Hospital. He suggested she see a surgeon for further investigations. Professor Nixon, who examined her and felt a large lump on the right side of her pelvis, recommended immediate and urgent surgery to investigate the lump. It was scheduled in three days' time. It must have been terrifying waiting but Rosalind busied herself writing letters detailing the results of her work at the Virus Lab in Berkeley and to thank the Rockefeller Foundation for funding her trip.

The surgery on 4 September revealed the worst possible news: she was suffering from ovarian cancer, with a tumour the size of a tennis ball in each ovary.

CANCER

Cancer is not a rare disease. Around forty per cent of people will have a cancerous growth at some point in their lives, though treatments are better than ever, if they are detected early enough. Some cancers are more dangerous than others, depending on how quick they are to grow and spread.

Cancer works at a cellular level. In a healthy human body, cells divide and copy themselves and new cells replace old ones, which die off naturally. Cancer is a disruption of this process and cells copy themselves inaccurately and do not stop copying when they should. The mass of malfunctioning cells is called a tumour. They can invade other tissues and cancerous cells can spread through the body.

A Dark Diagnosis

A well-known cause of many cancers is radiation, which directly damages DNA. Radiation was known to be dangerous before Rosalind was working with X-rays but safety procedures in the 1940s and 50s were a lot less strict than today. It's been documented that Rosalind was often less than careful when carrying out her experiments, spending longer than she was supposed to in the presence of X-ray beams and not always wearing the correct lead apron to protect herself from exposure to radiation. This doesn't mean that her X-ray work was definitely the cause of her illness – there's really no way to be sure. There was also a history of various cancers in her family, though in those days the disease wasn't widely talked about. Over the course of her research, she had regular doctor's visits to look for signs of radiation-caused sickness. She'd had one such check-up a couple of months before going to America and her doctor had noticed nothing of concern.

Some cancers are more obvious than others from the start of their growth. Some are detectable early, through lumps or other symptoms. Others lurk and grow and are only found much too late. Sadly for Rosalind, ovarian cancer was one of the latter, known as the "silent killer".

But her cancer hadn't defeated her yet. A month after her first operation, she had another, just to be sure the doctors had removed all the cancerous growths. By the end of these procedures Rosalind had undergone a full hysterectomy – the removal of her womb and ovaries. It would mean that she could never have children naturally.

While getting better from the operation, Rosalind moved into her parents' new house in Hampstead, rather than going back to her own flat in South Kensington. Though in recent years her mother and father had barely understood the complexities of her work, they understood cancer. Her mother often found it hard to hold back her tears, even though Rosalind herself was optimistic about a recovery. This wasn't just an act for the sake of her family and friends. Rosalind repeatedly wrote letters saying she hoped to be back to full strength and working soon and she continued to keep in touch with her work at Birkbeck. She approached her own cancer like a scientific problem that could be solved if the right steps were followed. The surgery was the first of those steps. There was no point worrying until more data came in.

Few people outside her family and oldest friends even knew she had cancer. Some knew she was ill and having treatment, which explained her not being at the lab as much as before, but that was all. When she was well enough to go to work, she seemed as bright and engaged as before she left for America. But for someone who was known as a workaholic, Rosalind's absences were noted. Even from Harvard in Boston, James Watson wrote that he "heard rumours she was not well" and wished her "a speedy return to health".

Rosalind didn't behave like someone who was worried about illness. She bought a brand-new car (the first she had owned), which she drove to the Birkbeck lab and her team continued their pioneering work on viruses. There was still a question mark over the future funding of the group though. Slater at the ARC had made it clear her grant from them would cease in around six months, so she submitted her application to the US National Institutes of Health. Eager to impress them, she explained in her application that they had seen some similarities between the spherical structure of some plant viruses to that of polio, a virus known to cause paralysis in children.

While she waited for the results, she took a well-earned break to Europe, visiting her old friends the Luzzatis, who now lived in Strasbourg, France with their young children. They had no idea she was ill. It seemed she was on the mend.

False Hopes

As 1957 began, Rosalind was having frequent check-ups at University College Hospital but no actual treatment. Sometimes she seemed quite well, but other times she suffered from sleepless nights and a lack of energy that meant she could only spend a few hours in the lab at a time. In April, the ARC renewed her grant for one more year. The team was safe for now, but Slater made it clear that there would be no further renewal – Rosalind would have to source a grant from elsewhere.

The lab work was incredibly fruitful. During 1956 they'd published several papers, many in the prestigious *Nature* and more were on the way in 1957. But late April brought things to a halt.

Rosalind was readmitted to hospital with severe stomach pains. Doctors had found another lump and this time they were brutally honest with her: she was dying.

Rosalind may have been positive around others but she was also a realist. She knew now that it was a matter of when, not if. For her, it was about extending the time she had left. She chose to have a new treatment called "cobalt radiotherapy", which involved firing gamma rays at a cancerous mass to kill the cells. It meant she had to frequently visit the hospital for treatment. Still, she didn't tell her colleagues where she was going and why, but those around her must have begun to guess it was more than a passing illness.

Even when undergoing radiotherapy, Rosalind kept up with her work engagements, giving lectures on her research and on X-ray techniques throughout the summer of 1957.

Her team's discoveries relating to the tobacco mosaic virus were about to become more widely known outside the world of scientific journals. Rosalind was contacted by the University of

Chicago's Professor, James William Moulder, who was handling the science section at the following year's Brussels World's Fair (or Expo 58, as it was known). This grand exhibition was taking place in the Belgian capital and was intended to showcase the best achievements from every nation, each of which had its own exhibition. It ran for six months and had over forty million visitors.

Part of the science section of Expo 58 focused on viruses. Moulder wanted Rosalind and the Birkbeck team to build a giant model of the tobacco mosaic virus and the turnip yellow mosaic virus. Though she was ill, Rosalind relished the challenge.

Her spirits were lifted further when Caspar arrived, with his mother, at Cambridge. She took them for a picnic in Richmond Park and even had the widowed Mrs Caspar to stay at her London flat for several days. Rosalind continued to socialize with the Cricks too. None of them were aware of the severity of her illness and Crick continued to honestly criticize her work where he thought it could be improved.

He thought that she was rushing to publish certain papers before they were ready and found the behaviour unusual in someone who was normally so cautious. Rosalind had good reason – the more she could show her team were engaged in important findings, the more likely their futures would be secured after her death. And it seemed to work because her application to the US National Institutes of Health was approved. The grant of £10,000 a year for three years was for the work, not her personally, so it wouldn't matter if she wasn't there to spend it.

The lump in her pelvis wasn't showing signs of shrinking under the frequent blasts of gamma rays. Against the advice of the hospital, Rosalind travelled to Europe once more that summer. She and Caspar attended a conference on the polio virus in Switzerland, then visited the mountainous region of Zermatt. She no longer had the strength to climb the hills but as Casper's elderly mother was accompanying them, it wasn't noticed.

She then went to Paris, for a protein conference, before a long driving holiday with her sister Jenifer in northern Italy.

Jenifer later wrote that their father had told her to "make it as good a holiday as I could for Rosalind".

Rosalind appreciated seeing the wonderful countryside. There was already a sense of what she was losing though. She would rather have been on foot, with "rucksacks and tents" than in "a little tin box", as she called Jenifer's Morris Minor car.

The Last Battle

When Rosalind returned to Birkbeck in autumn 1957, she began work on polio, using samples of the crystallized virus supplied from Berkeley, California. Though Bernal was comfortable with the idea, the research caused some tension at Birkbeck among some of the other staff. The labs at Torrington Square already had a reputation as being quite run down and the thought of handling a potentially deadly virus there worried some. What if it was accidentally released?

POLIO

Polio (or poliomyelitis to give its full name) is an infectious virus that can cause a range of symptoms, some more severe than others, from headaches to temporary loss of sensation in the limbs, paralysis and even death.

It has been around for thousands of years and is known to affect children particularly badly. In 1950, there were around 7,500 cases of polio paralysis in the UK and 750 deaths. People with ill-formed limbs due to polio paralysis were a common sight.

Scientists in the United States developed a vaccine in 1952, which severely reduced the number of cases, but the UK was slower to follow with its own effective vaccination programme.

It wasn't until the 1980s that polio was completely eradicated in the UK.

John Bernal and Rosalind tried to reassure everyone that the virus would be contained. They eventually agreed to store the samples at the London School of Hygiene and Tropical Medicine and that every necessary precaution would be taken with the samples when they were being transported and analysed. In fact, the risks were minimal. Rosalind didn't bother to take the polio vaccine prior to working with the virus. Not because she was unafraid of contracting the disease but because she was confident she could handle the samples without putting herself at risk.

As autumn turned to winter, her illness worsened. She was now under the care of a specialist cancer hospital, the Royal Marsden, where she began chemotherapy. The doctors told her that she had no chance of recovery and the news both angered and saddened her. She was a scientist who'd always looked for solutions to the most difficult problems. A close friend wrote of the time: "She was indignant that there was not the technical skill available to avert death." While she was being treated, she remained at the hospital in a private room. Her family regularly came to see her and she had a constant stream of visitors. News of Rosalind's illness began to spread more widely. It was left to Aaron Klug to complete the models for the Brussels World's Fair.

TREATMENTS FOR CANCER

Where radiotherapy attempts to "kill" cancer cells with radiation, chemotherapy is a treatment in which chemicals are introduced to the body to poison the cells. It often has much more severe side effects, such as nausea, hair loss and weight loss, because it cannot target cancer cells as directly as radiation.

As the chemotherapy continued, Rosalind's physical state deteriorated. She became too weak to look after herself and so moved out of her parents' house and in with her brother, Roland. This was partly to spare her mother and father seeing her condition but also because she liked having her nieces and nephews around.

Around this time, Rosalind wrote her will, leaving large sums of money to Aaron Klug and her physician friend, Dr Mair Livingstone, and Anne Crawford, a friend from her days at St Paul's. She also left money to Ada Griffiths, or "Nannie", and instructions that the rest of her estate be given to charity.

The creation of a will did not mean Rosalind felt she was going to die soon. She continued to make arrangements for the future, including holidays in Vienna and the United States, as well as buying tickets to the Faraday Society Conference in Leeds in April. There were even plans to move the team to the Cavendish Laboratory in Cambridge, now under Max Perutz, to continue their research in a more up-to-date setting.

But Rosalind sadly didn't live to see these plans put into action. As the end neared, her determination grew. Even in her severely weakened state, she put in long days at Torrington Square. Occasionally, she had to crawl up the stairs to get to her labs because she wasn't strong enough to walk and refused help. The sight of it made members of her team cry. There were better moments though, when she managed to socialize at the homes of friends, or go for very short walks.

Two days after her father's sixty-fourth birthday, at which she ate well but looked ill, she took a turn for the worse. Her aunt took her back to the Royal Marsden for what would be the final time. There, an operation revealed that the cancer had spread throughout her body. There was nothing to be done but make her comfortable. Rosalind was unable to eat properly or lift her head. Jacques Mering came to visit and her skeletal appearance brought him to tears.

Rosalind deteriorated over a two-week period and died on 16 April. It was the same day that *The Times* newspaper carried a report on her TMV model at the Brussels World's Fair. Rosalind's funeral was held at a Jewish Cemetery, attended by family, friends and scientists.

She was buried among her ancestors in the Franklin family plot.

A LASTING LEGACY

Under her name, Rosalind's gravestone reads: "Scientist: her research and discoveries on viruses remain of lasting benefit to mankind." It seems like quite a brief summary for a remarkable life and barely covers her enormous contributions to science. It's challenging even to guess at what she could have achieved if she had lived longer but it's fair to say that with another thirty years, she would almost certainly have become a much more famous figure than she is today. John Bernal, her long-time boss, wrote accounts of her life in both *The Times* and *Nature*, in which he covered the variety of her work and heaped praise upon her. In the latter, he writes: "As a scientist Miss Franklin was distinguished by extreme clarity and perfection in everything she undertook. Her photographs are among the most beautiful X-ray photographs of any substance ever taken." Rosalind would have appreciated the simple honesty and respect from a fellow scientist.

Of course, she is known today mostly for one particular area of study. The work done by Rosalind Franklin, Francis Crick, James Watson, Maurice Wilkins, Ray Gosling and many others, explained for the first time the structure of DNA. This later made it possible to understand how cells copy information through an organism and how parents pass on their genes to their offspring.

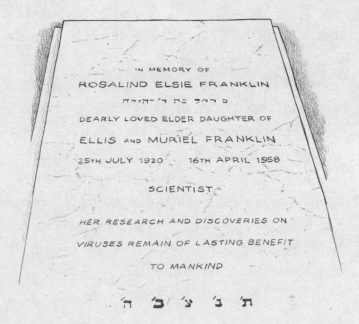

IN MEMORY OF

ROSALIND ELSIE FRANKLIN

רחל פה בת ר' יהודה

DEARLY LOVED ELDER DAUGHTER OF

ELLIS AND MURIEL FRANKLIN

25TH JULY 1920   16TH APRIL 1958

SCIENTIST

HER RESEARCH AND DISCOVERIES ON

VIRUSES REMAIN OF LASTING BENEFIT

TO MANKIND

ת נ צ ב' ה

All in the Genes

Our understanding of genetics has improved a lot in the years after Rosalind's death and we are currently in the midst of a genetic revolution. The Human Genome Project was launched in 1990 in order to map the full genome of a human being – that is the entire strand of their DNA, including around three billion base pairs. It took thirteen years, hundreds of scientists and around $2.7 billion to complete. Today, the same process takes around a day, costs about $1,000 and can be carried out with one technician and a computer.

Scientists estimate that we have around 20,000 to 25,000 genes (sections of DNA) in each cell, bundled into chromosomes, and we've only just started to understand how those genes operate to cause things like physical or psychological traits or diseases. In some cases, single genes cause obvious outcomes but in most, scientists believe our genes and our environment combine to produce physical changes.

THE FUTURE

For millions of years, the human genome has evolved by accident. Tiny changes in our genes that occur naturally have either been passed on if we have children, or die, if we do not. But that mechanism of what Darwin called "natural selection" is changing.

We are beginning to explore how we can change our genes artificially, either by introducing new strands of DNA or removing harmful ones. This process is called "gene therapy". We already genetically modify food and plants, such as making fruit skin thinner, or making crops more resistant to disease and we genetically engineer animals in labs to experiment with better medicines for humans. This is just the first stage of the genetic revolution.

To many people, this sounds frightening. And we are right to be cautious. Humans have always pushed technology and science to their very limits. But the genetically modified future that we're rushing towards is a place of great potential too. It could hold the answer to feeding the population of the world, to getting rid of genetic diseases or disabilities and slowing the aging process. And it all stems back to a simple idea – the double helix structure of DNA.

Remembering Rosalind

Though Rosalind didn't receive a great fanfare at the time of the discovery, today the wider scientific community recognizes her huge contribution. She might not have been awarded a Nobel Prize along with Crick, Watson and Wilkins but there are labs, buildings and institutions named after her around the world, including at St Paul's, Birkbeck, King's and Cambridge, the institutions where she studied and worked.

Along with numerous awards and fellowships named in her honour, the European Space Agency even called a Mars Rover "Rosalind Franklin". In 2015, Anna Ziegler's play, *Photograph 51*, was staged in London and featured Rosalind, Gosling, Wilkins, Crick and Watson.

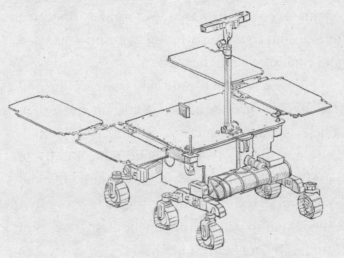

However, recognition of her importance was slow to come. The most famous account of the race to discover the structure of DNA comes from James Watson's memoir, *The Double Helix*. In it, Rosalind (or "Rosy", as he insisted on calling her) is painted as hard to work with and unattractive. But Watson himself comes across as very sexist and arrogant.

Harvard University Press were originally going to publish the book but had so many complaints, before it was even published, from the individuals mentioned in it (including his friends Crick, Pauling, Wilkins, Randall and Bernal) that the publisher decided not to go ahead. One of the common complaints was Watson's unfair treatment of Rosalind Franklin, who by that time was dead and couldn't defend herself.

However, another publisher stepped in and *The Double Helix* became an instant bestseller. There was still plenty of criticism though and later in life, Watson spoke more kindly of Franklin, admitting his words as a young man no longer reflected his true feelings. He was often called upon to defend the way he and Crick used Rosalind's data behind her back.

For a long time, Rosalind Franklin was remembered for her missed opportunities. She is often criticized for not being imaginative enough to see the structure of DNA that her own data suggested. Others say she was stubborn or unable to work in a team. These criticisms seem deeply unfair. Though there may have been occasions where she clashed with colleagues, those incidents were few and far between. The evidence suggests that she really had no problem with collaboration. She worked successfully with Jacques Mering, with Ray Gosling, and later researched with Aaron Klug and Don Caspar. They describe her as a fearless and hard-working experimentalist. If she was stubborn at times, she had to be in order to be heard. There were many times she could have become discouraged in her career but she pressed on regardless. She brought the same determination to the lab that she took on her hiking adventures. If she had followed her father's advice at the age of nineteen and left university, there's no way of knowing where she would have ended up.

Rosalind approached her life as if she knew it would be short, or at least aware of how easy it would be to get distracted. Even if she never complained about sexism, she must have seen how few female scientists there were and would have realized the hostile attitudes she sometimes faced because of that. Her blunt manner could well have been a reaction to this – if she was going to prove herself, it had to be on their terms; she knew her science had to be flawless. Interestingly, when she began to see real success studying viruses at Birkbeck, touring America, few people commented negatively about her prickliness. It seems when she was confident in herself, having earned respect, she took her armour off.

Rosalind's legacy isn't just the content of her work and her discoveries. By proving herself in a male-dominated field, she paved the way for generations of women after her to prosper in the sciences. In Rosalind's time, one in ten undergraduates at Cambridge were female and they could attend only two colleges. In 2019, young women outnumber men in the biological sciences at the same university and all the colleges accept female students.

Rosalind never had children or a romantic partner. Her friend Anne Sayre said that Rosalind was in love with Don Caspar, whom she met towards the end of her short life but if she ever told him so, we do not know. She was certainly in love with their work. It may be that she feared marriage and children would prevent her working – to be a successful scientist in the 1940s and 50s relied on publishing regular papers.

One of the men she respected greatly was Francis Crick. They could criticize each other without offence. After her death, even though he had been her friend, Crick did speak about her in many of the same terms as others. He called her "oversensitive", unable to accept advice and "prickly". But rather than being unintuitive he thought that perhaps she, "mistrusted ... her intuition." This might be closer to the truth because, for Rosalind, her branch of science wasn't about intuition at all. Just as her way of looking at the world wasn't through a lens of faith or traditional values or nationalistic politics, she dealt from the start in things she could see and measure and experience firsthand. She formed opinions of people based on their behaviour, not their reputations and positions or class. There were no mysteries, because she could design experiments to expose them. There was no reason to guess because the answers were there if she looked hard enough. She was never content to skirt the bottoms of mountains, imagining their peaks; they had to be climbed.

TIMELINE OF ROSALIND FRANKLIN'S LIFE

1920 Rosalind Franklin is born on 25 July

1938 Begins studying chemistry at Newnham College, Cambridge

1941 Graduates with Second Class Honours in chemistry

1945 Publishes her thesis, *The physical chemistry of solid organic colloids, with special reference to the structure of coal and related materials*

1946 Moves to Paris to continue studies of coal under Jacques Mering

1951 Begins working as a research associate at King's College London

1952 Rosalind takes Photograph 51

1953 Watson and Crick publish their findings on the structure of DNA

1953 Rosalind leaves King's College and joins J D Bernal's team at Birkbeck, studying viruses

1956 Rosalind is diagnosed with ovarian cancer

1958 Rosalind dies on 16 April

1962 Watson and Crick receive Nobel Prize in Medicine

BIBLIOGRAPHY AND FURTHER READING

Glynn, Jenifer (2012)
My Sister Rosalind Franklin: A Family Memoir
Oxford University Press

Maddox, Brenda (2002)
The Dark Lady of DNA
HarperCollins

Sayre, Anne (1975)
Rosalind Franklin and DNA
W. W. Norton & Company

Watson, James (1968)
The Double Helix: A Personal Account of the Discovery of the Structure of DNA
Weidenfeld & Nicolson

Ziegler, Anna (2015)
Photograph 51 (play)

GLOSSARY

Aplastic anaemia: deficiency of all types of blood cell caused by failure of bone marrow development

Arrondissement: a district of Paris; there are twenty arrondissements in the city

Atom: the basic building block for all matter in the universe, made up of tiny particles called protons, neutrons and electrons

Base pairs: the name given to the combinations of nucleobases (guanine, adenine, cytosine, thymine) that link the two halves of a DNA strand

Capsomeres: an outer covering of protein that protects the genetic material of a virus

Carbon: a chemical element which has two main forms (diamond and graphite) and which also occurs in impure form in charcoal, soot and coal

Cell: the smallest structural unit of an organism

Chromosome: a threadlike structure of nucleic acids and protein found in the nucleus of most living cells, carrying genetic information in the form of genes

Crystallography: the branch of science concerned with the structure and properties of crystals

Darkroom: a room for developing photographs frm film, from which normal light is excluded

Degree: a mark awarded to a university student to show they've completed their course

Diffraction: the process by which a beam of light or other radiation is bent as a result of passing around atoms

DNA: deoxyribonucleic acid, a self-replicating material present in nearly all living organisms; carrier of genetic information

Gender inequality: giving a group of people different opportunities due to perceived differences based solely on gender

Gene: a strand of DNA in a chromosome that forms unit of heredity which is transferred from a parent organism to its offspring

Genome: the complete set of genes or genetic material present in a cell or organism

Grant: a sum of money given by a government or other organization for a particular purpose

Helix: an object having a three-dimensional shape like that of a wire wound around a cylinder, like a corkscrew or spiral staircase

Heredity: the passing on of physical or mental characteristics genetically from one generation to another

Mineralogy: the study of minerals, solid substances that are formed naturally in the earth

Molecule: a group of atoms bonded together

Nobel Prize: any of six international prizes awarded annually for outstanding work in physics, chemistry, physiology or medicine, literature, economics and the promotion of peace

Nucleic acid molecule: long chainlike molecules composed of a series of nearly identical building blocks called nucleotides

Optics: the scientific study of the behaviour of light and other forms of electromagnetic radiation

Organic: relating to living matter; containing carbon

Organism: an individual animal, plant or other life form

Pacifism: the belief that disputes should be settled by peaceful means and that violence should never be used

PhD: the highest level university degree, after which a person can be called a doctor; also called a doctorate

Polymer: a large molecule, composed of many repeated molecular units

Prejudice: an unreasonable opinion or dislike that is not based on reason or experience

Propaganda: false or exaggerated information, used to win support for a political cause or point of view

Protein: an acid molecule that has a variety of functions within an organism

Radiation: the emission of energy as electromagnetic waves; visible light and X-rays are both forms of radiation

Royal Institution: an organization devoted to scientific education and research, based in London. It was founded in 1799 by the leading British scientists of the age

Royal Society: a group of leading scientists founded in the seventeenth century

Synagogue: a building in which people of Jewish faith meet for religious worship or teaching

Thesis: a long essay or dissertation involving personal research, written by a candidate for a university degree

Treaty: a written agreement between different countries

Undergraduate: a student who is undertaking a degree and has not yet graduated

Union of Soviet Socialist Republics (USSR): a former communist country in eastern Europe and northern Asia that lasted from 1924 to 1991

Virus: an infectious agent that typically consists of a nucleic acid molecule in a protein coat. Too small to be seen by the naked eye, viruses are able to multiply only within the living cells of a host

X-ray: an electromagnetic wave of high energy and very short wavelength, which is able to pass through many materials that normal light cannot penetrate

INDEX

WHY NOT READ
KATHERINE JOHNSON BY
LEILA RASHEED...

KATHERINE JOHNSON

There will always be SCIENCE, ENGINEERING and TECHNOLOGY.

And there will always, always be MATHEMATICS

A LiFE STORY

NASA Mathematician

WHY NOT READ
STEPHEN HAWKING BY
NIKKI SHEEHAN...

STEPHEN HAWKING

Without IMPERFECTION, neither YOU nor I would EXIST.

Theoretical Physicist

WHY NOT READ
ALAN TURING BY
JOANNA NADIN...

ALAN TURING

I propose to consider the question, 'Can machines think?'

A LiFE STORY

Computer Scientist

NOTES

....

....

....

....

....

....

....

....

....

....